MW00387116

Kim Miller

REdesigning churches

CREATING SPACES FOR
CONNECTION AND COMMUNITY

 Abingdon Press™

Nashville

REDESIGNING CHURCHES

CREATING SPACES FOR CONNECTION AND COMMUNITY

Copyright © 2013 by Abingdon Press

All rights reserved.

No part of this work may be reproduced or transmitted in any form or by any means, electronic or mechanical, including photocopying and recording, or by any information storage or retrieval system, except as may be expressly permitted by the 1976 Copyright Act or in writing from the publisher. Requests for permission can be addressed to Permissions, The United Methodist Publishing House, P.O. Box 801, 201 Eighth Avenue South, Nashville, TN 37202-0801, or e-mailed to permissions@umpublishing.org.

Library of Congress Cataloging-in-Publication Data

Miller, Kim, 1956-
   Redesigning churches : creating spaces for connection and community /
Kim Miller.
      pages cm
   ISBN 978-1-4267-5792-1 (pbk., adhesive perfect binding : alk. paper)
1. Church architecture. 2. Liturgy and architecture. 3. Church facilities—Planning. I. Title.
   NA4810.M55 2013
   254'.7—dc23

                                                                                    2013032731

Unless otherwise noted, scripture quotations are from the Common English Bible. Copyright © 2011 by the Common English Bible. All rights reserved. Used by permission. www.CommonEnglishBible.com.

Scripture quotations marked *THE MESSAGE* are taken from *THE MESSAGE*. Copyright © by Eugene H. Peterson 1993, 1994, 1995, 1996, 2000, 2001, 2002. Used by permission of NavPress Publishing Group.

The headings in this book are set in Rock Salt, ©Apache.org (http://www.fontsquirrel.com/license/rock-salt).

13 14 15 16 17 18 19 20 21 22—10 9 8 7 6 5 4 3 2 1
MANUFACTURED IN THE UNITED STATES OF AMERICA

DEDICATION

To Linkin, Amari, Kenyon, Anthem, Beatrice, and Boston:
May your bursting creativity be exceeded only by your confidence to attempt the impossible;
great dreams toward an eternal purpose—amen.

CONTENTS

PART I
DIVINE DESIGN 1

PART II
MAKEOVER MOMENTUM: THE WHO, WHAT, AND HOW OF NINE MAKEOVER PROJECTS 23

PART III
STEEPLES TO STARBUCKS: REIMAGINING WORSHIP SPACES 49

PART IV
STAGE DESIGN 65

Acknowledgments

A dream doesn't become reality through magic; it takes sweat, determination, and hard work.

—Colin Powell

Creating spaces for connection and community is really the story of my own community connections. Without the teams surrounding the dreams there would be no book, no chronicling of *ReDesigning Churches*.

Heartfelt gratitude goes out to the leadership team of Ginghamsburg Church. Mike Slaughter, Karen Smith, Nate Gibson, and Dave Hood—you trust me way too much. Thanks for frequently empowering beyond what makes sense at the time.

Kudos to our worship design and media teams. I would be crazy to take credit for what you guys bring to life so faithfully every single weekend. Working with all of you keeps me focused and keeps me laughing. Shout out to Lindsay Hefner for her gorgeous photography and to Dan Bracken for the consistent creation of beautiful worship series graphics—talent in motion.

The Ginghamsburg makeover team is much more than a team—you are my homies, my community, my posse. You roll with the crazy ideas and work so hard to build and breathe life into our campus spaces. I'm so proud of each and every one of you for serving till it hurts and staying until it's done.

My life-group "sistas" are the real deal. You ladies are the ultimate Designing Women, the best listeners, advisers, cooks, and creators this side of IKEA, and I love how our stories interweave makeover mania with laughter and love.

Last but so not least, huge props go out to my partner in creation, Clark Miller. Not only did we make three remarkable kids of our own, we've also managed a life full of amazing projects as a team—and you're still making my greatest makeover dreams come true.

INTRODUCTION

A Whole New World

It was a very hot morning in July—90 degrees and counting. Mike and Carolyn Slaughter, Ginghamsburg's lead pastor and his wife, had invited our worship design team to convene at their North Carolina cabin for three days of fun, connection, and visioning forward together. We had pontoon boats reserved for the afternoon excursion on Lake Chatuge, but—first things first—the morning would hold intense starter discussions about how we saw God leading us into the fall.

Mike began with a spiritual entrepreneur's devotional—the kind that always engages me. He explained how two years before, BlackBerry had the cell-phone market wrapped up tight. Everyone wanted a BlackBerry because it offered the beauty of a texting cell phone along with instant e-mail, a modest camera, and a few other features thrown in. Easy to use and all the rage (mine was pink and I loved it!), that little device had friends and family dubbing us "CrackBerries."

"Trouble is," Mike continued, "BlackBerry didn't account for two things: our thirst to see our information in pictures and our desire to navigate using a touch screen." Now I don't know about you, but I can't really remember much about life before I was able to see my friends' lives illustrated play by play—much of it through pictures and graphics. It's as though we were created to experience life in color, not simply through the black-on-white text that once held its own.

I'm not sure what everyone else on the team was thinking that morning, but for Kim Miller, another lightbulb had just illuminated my world. "That's my metaphor," I heard myself say. "The iPhone (or Droid or insert Smartphone of your choice) is to the cell-phone world as space design is to ministry."

Humans live and work in environments, and we thrive in creative spaces. We are tuned in to visuals all around us. We drink in the beauty of the world, love when our senses are engaged, and best experience life in the context of environments that point to the One who "fearfully and wonderfully made" every human on the planet. We were created to engage with the world around us.

New Conversations

The church of Jesus is engaging in all new conversations. When I first entered the ministry world, most churches were arguing over music preferences, dress code, and rebellious youth-group behaviors. Today the majority of faith communities have grown to understand stylistic preferences in worship. We seldom attach spiritual significance to wardrobe, and we count ourselves blessed if and when teens find their way through our church doors at all. The landscape of ministry has changed, for sure.

A new dialogue is emerging, and we find ourselves in the midst of a freshly complex season of ministry, carrying the gospel into our fast-changing world in the best ways we know how. No longer a performance-based gathering, vital worship must be an engaging, inspiring, and infectious dialogue; we must lose our spectator paradigm and move in the direction of contagious community.

Complexities abound, however, and current challenges can be traced to relevance: How can we be the contagious and vital presence of Jesus to a world that yearns for spiritual connection? How will we meet the myriad immediate and long-term needs of the "least of these" in our neighborhoods and beyond? And how might the aging structures we inhabit be reimagined toward kingdom growth and vitality? Is it possible to create new skins for the new wine of our missional communities?

Thinking new thoughts about old paradigms is not for the faint of heart. We become emotionally attached to inanimate objects and to ways of doing things. Sometimes outside objective voices can help name what at the deepest level we know to be true. Being open to new ideas is risky and fearful at best, yet at the juncture of every crazy, faith-testing step, Jesus was quick to verbalize this life mantra: *Don't be afraid.*

Perhaps this is exactly where you find your own church community—ready to move forward, the reality of the need for a fresh wind of the Spirit to blow through your walls intensified by the more visual and tactile aspects of your building environments. As we embark on this current missional challenge, let's confront head-on the needs of the present and build with confident faith into all the possibilities that God's best future holds.

Inspired Design: My Story

My own journey into environmental awareness is a bit convoluted. I can only trace through the seasons of my life and series of passions. As a child, my broken family environment often left me alone to think and dream *What if?* In the midst of this relational chaos, I discovered that there was one thing I could actually control, one activity whereby I could impose change into my daily situation at home, and that was my physical environment. Even as a ten-year-old, I discovered that rearranging the furniture in my own room every week could afford me a brand-new environment. Creating a different "world" from time to time (no doubt to escape the painful reality of my outside world) engaged my ideation, changed my perspective, and became an art form I have continued to enjoy practicing throughout my life—even after the world became a much more manageable place.

Occasionally my grandparents would visit, or we would visit their small home. These family gatherings were happier times, and I remember overhearing conversations between my mom and her mom while they sat in my grandmother's living room—which was a remodeled one-room schoolhouse—talking through all the possibilities a furnished room could offer. They were always mentally arranging and rearranging things, and then they would share their ideas with each other.

"We could put the piano on that south wall, Marian."

"But where would we put Great-grandma's hutch?"

"Well, it could move around to the wall over next to the window. The light would still flow in real nice."

"I never thought of that! Still, the old secretary would need to go. It's been crowded ever since you brought that old thing out here."

"You're right. I'll get Daddy to move it back to the bedroom."

On and on they went. It was undoubtedly therapy for Depression-weary minds. I'd listen intently and try to picture each move they described right along with them. What that gentle banter taught me early on was that things could be rearranged. They can change. Despite our limited financial resources, we're not stuck here with the "same old, same old." We can make the very same room look totally different every single week if we want to. And I grew up thinking that everyone's family changed up the living room every week. Heck, it was good, cheap fun and awarded us a newish house each time the rearranging ensued. "All new day, all new chances!" Who could know that seeds were being sown to grow a ministry career around the concept that we can—and must!—reimagine our community environments to suit the needs of the occasion?

Imagine my dismay when years later I had my first encounter inside a traditional church building and found all the furniture in the sanctuary not only unmoved from week to week but also virtually bolted to the floor. That traditional church configuration spoke volumes to my spirit. It said, "We're committed to never changing this up; we must keep things exactly as they are week after week, year after year." "Someday, somehow, this will have to change," I promised myself.

My first years at Ginghamsburg Church were spent leading our worship design team, which is still very close to my heart. I have always enjoyed being part of the team that brings the Word to our people in fresh and creative ways week after week. All those years I was convinced that we were never simply designing worship, however. We were creating life-changing God experiences. All the details of integrating music, media, and messages, grounded in the truth of God's Word, served to provide environments for transformation. I will always be grateful for the many amazing moments watching God work in us and through us (and often in spite of us!).

All the while I was designing worship, however, I was also paying attention to my "drivers"—that is, what motivated me to get up and go to work each morning and what I enjoyed most about designing unique worship experiences week after week after week. More and more I found myself focusing on the environment. I'd become fascinated with the human ability to build worlds and name them, to design environments that evoked emotion and transported faith-seekers to a place intentionally crafted. Within the realm of our church world, we call these experiences "worship celebrations." We would name a direction for the spoken word, and I would proceed to crawl inside that message from scripture and ask, "How might it *feel* to be inside the four walls of the worship center, experiencing *this* word? How might we arrange our physical surroundings so that the ambience also communicates this one entirely new set of messages and distinguishes it from the last message series evoked?"

I began not only thinking about this while brainstorming with our team but also pursuing these concepts in my free time as well—while shopping, walking, traveling, or choosing reading material. It became my magnificent obsession. Beginning by staging events—funerals, dinners, pop-up shops, and coffee cafés—then moving on to stage design, I explored this propensity to create spaces for connection and community. In time I was invited to recruit an unpaid team to redesign and remodel a dated church building that Ginghamsburg had acquired as a satellite campus in Dayton, Ohio (Fort McKinley UMC). A few years later, I designed a second church-plant campus, this time a storefront in a shopping plaza.

It's fair to say that designing spaces for connection and community has become a way of living and breathing for me. I find myself impassioned by issues that others completely overlook and fanatical about concepts that others cannot yet see. The Old Testament book of Nehemiah chronicles his basic building strategy: he saw a vision, formed a plan, recruited a team, and oversaw the rebuilding of Jerusalem's broken walls. I'm convinced that just as Nehemiah worked that plan, God can still use servants possessing this passion for leading new kingdom construction. I believe God can be enjoyed and worshiped more fully as I dare to exercise this calling for God's glory. Consider what Thomas Merton had to say on the subject of "true vocation":

> Discovering vocation does not mean scrambling toward some prize just beyond my reach but accepting the treasure of true self I already possess. Vocation does not come from a voice "out there" calling me to be something I am not. It comes from a voice "in here" calling me to be the person I was born to be, to fulfill the original selfhood given me at birth by God. (quoted by Parker Palmer, www.inward/outward.com)

A second entry on vocation/calling in Parker Palmer's blog states:

> Our deepest calling is to grow into our own authentic selfhood, whether or not it conforms to some image of who we ought to be. As we do so, we will not only find the joy that every human being seeks—we will also find our path of authentic service in the world.
>
> True vocation joins self and service, as Frederick Buechner asserts when he defines vocation as "the place where your deep gladness meets the world's deep need." Buechner's definition starts with the self and moves toward the needs of the world: it begins, wisely, where vocation begins—not in what the world needs (which is everything), but in the nature of the human self, in what brings the self joy, the deep joy of knowing that we are here on earth to be the gifts that God created. (www.inwardoutward.org/2008/03/04/true-vocation)

We all "see" different things. Some clearly see other people (thank God for them). Others may see nature, animals, cars, or unusual happenings. When I walk into a room, I see and feel emotional space, and my mind goes to work rearranging it toward a desirable end. Andy Stanley, founder and pastor of North Point Ministries in Atlanta, Georgia, chronicled the strategy North Point Community Church used to create churches that unchurched people love to attend. The book is titled *Deep & Wide* (Grand Rapids: Zondervan, 2012), and in the chapter "Creating Irresistible Environments," Andy says this about church settings:

> The desire to create order from chaos is a vestige of the thumbprint of God on our souls. Some of us do that intuitively with numbers—others with organizations. And then there are those talented people who can do the same with physical space. God has gifted a subset of us with the ability to take a space and make it comfortable. Attractive. Appealing. I'm not one of those people. But I have made it a habit to make sure there are a bunch of them around me with their eyes on our environments. Why? I want our physical environments to be magnetic. Irresistible. (p. 165)

Whether for worship design or campus design, my call is to help uncover the human craving inside each of us that invites us to enjoy sights, smells, sounds, and tastes and to awaken the part of us that confirms our propensity to engage life through our senses.

This might be a good place to pause a moment and let me ask a few questions: Do people entering your church spaces have to put their best senses into their back pockets when they arrive on your campus? And what era does your campus environment whisper that your church family is living in? Where are you on the "design map"? What is your story?

What Is Your Story?

I've observed that most people—including pastors—are one of three style types. See if you can identify yourself below:

- You appreciate intentional design but could be happy living in a warm cave.

- You love the design world but are dependent on others to implement changes.

- You completely embrace the world of environment and design and strive to implement richness of experience wherever you go.

What Is Your Earliest Church Multisensory Experience?

No matter where you are on the design map, your experience of faith and community has been greatly affected and remembered through your historic environments. Our spaces significantly color our feelings and receptivity to God's spirit, which is one reason I'm passionate about using this tool for kingdom connection.

Even now, the desire to connect people to God through worship draws me in. In my earlier book, *Redesigning Worship: Creating Powerful God Experiences*, the emphasis was on the combination of learning and feelings in our weekly gathering moments, realizing that our humanness allows us to process information in multiple ways at the same time. "God experiences" vary in nature, location, and demographic, but we all must have them in order to know love and hope and direction and meaning in our lives.

Adam and Eve encountered God after eating the forbidden fruit. Abraham heard a word from God just as the ax was to come down on his son Isaac. Moses experienced God calling to him from a flaming bush. David had a heart-wrenching God experience as he repented of his own deep sin.

When talking about true life change, people tend to speak about a message they heard and an *experience* they had. I want to believe that it is possible for all of us to have powerful God experiences. While designers cannot make that happen in the context of our weekly worship celebrations or in the casual atmosphere of our community spaces, we can certainly prepare a generously inviting collection of spaces where God can powerfully show up. Once we've prepared, we can step back and allow the Holy Spirit to move and to create God's best work in people's lives.

Getting Started

When it comes right down to it, all projects—especially God projects—require leadership. Great leadership will make all the difference in any ministry endeavor. If this is your calling, you will be the one to remind people of what it is you are striving to build and why it matters. You will be the one painting a picture of engaging environments. And God will use you to ennoble and empower others to rest assured that if God has called you to it, God will see you through it. We can do this together!

As you read and process these stories of redesign, my prayer is that you will find renewed inspiration for the great vision of creating your own engaging environments, that you will gain more ideas than you can possibly use in one lifetime, and that you'll discover the courage to achieve all God is calling you and your team to do in Jesus' name. So let's get started.

PART 1

DIVINE DESIGN

In the beginning, the earth was like an unpainted, poorly lit room with all the furniture in boxes in the hallway waiting to be assembled and properly arranged. So God started rearranging the furniture.

—*Andy Stanley,* Deep & Wide

One reason I was attracted to Ginghamsburg Church was the attention to detail I noted when I first arrived at worship that Sunday in 1993. Not only was casual attire the norm, but guests were allowed to bring their mugs of hot coffee into the worship area. This was unheard of at the time but spoke volumes to me about this unique faith community. The message was that I could be the same person inside the church walls as I was outside the church. This was a place that found a way to integrate sacred and secular, as evidenced by this one hospitable permission (and a few radio songs they played on the side).

It was Advent season in the early 1990s, and my young family was new to Ginghamsburg Church. My husband and I told each other we were there to "hide and heal" after a very rough patch in another ministry setting. Sitting in worship in the crowded Discipleship Center (located on what is now Ginghamsburg's South Campus), I happened to notice that a lightbulb in the garland encircling the room was burned out. This bothered my obsessive self, but I seriously doubted it bothered anyone else—after all, I was in a church and was quite used to being put off by things that no one else seemed to notice, especially in church environments. On that day, however, I found company in my disturbance. Between worship celebrations, the young man who had been running sound in the back of the room sidled up to that green garland and screwed in a brand-new bulb—voilà, lights uninterrupted! What joy! This could be my church after all.

You see, what I know now is that how our church buildings are cared for, how the gardens are weeded, how the glass shines, how the spaces are intentionally designed—these details all whisper to human guests that they will or will not be cared for. It's really the only manual we have on such matters as we enter a space for the very first time. As church leaders, we must consider our relationship with those we seek to serve: men, women, students, infants, grandparents, and the lost and oppressed along with the rich and famous. We must lift a vision for the way life can look. Missiologist Michael Frost asserts, "Our true calling from God is to wipe the grime from the window [of life], allowing the light of Christ to dispel the darkness—and to reveal the beauty and goodness of God to a hurting world." New pictures and hope for our lives and locations and a haven of hospitality in the midst of all sorts of brokenness—this is the call I've found as my own.

GOD IN THE DETAILS

The fact that we're bastions of boredom rather than bursting with creativity and the release of the arts is such an embarrassment. We should be the place that is known for creativity as we have a direct connection to the Creator.

—*Leonard Sweet*

Did you know that twelve of the forty chapters of Exodus are devoted to aesthetics, that is, to precise details about altars and oils and offerings and everything in between? God had a wildly creative and multisensory image of how it was to be there in the holy of holies, and—let's be clear—the details mattered:

> Have them make an acacia-wood chest. It should be forty-five inches long, twenty-seven inches wide, and twenty-seven inches high. Cover it with pure gold, inside and out, and make a gold molding all around it. Cast four gold rings for it and put them on its four feet, two rings on one side and two rings on the other. Make acacia-wood poles and cover them with gold. Then put the poles into the rings on the chest's sides and use them to carry the chest. The poles should stay in the chest's rings. They shouldn't be taken out of them. Put the covenant document that I will give you into the chest. (Exodus 25:10-16)

Some say that 1 percent of what we do makes 99 percent of the difference. Attention to detail is not a new thought. Artists of all disciplines have discovered the difference between mediocre and amazing:

> To create something exceptional, your mind-set must be relentlessly focused on the smallest detail. (Giorgio Armani, Italian-born fashion designer)

> The difference between something good and something great is attention to detail. (Charles R. Swindoll, educator and radio pastor)

> God is in the details. (Ludwig Mies van der Rohe, German-born American architect)

And although attention to the details in design, architecture, and basic housekeeping is extremely important, it's really about the potential of what can happen within the walls of these intentionally crafted spaces. Great design—and our subsequent calling—is not to impress our guests with all our dazzling efforts but to prepare places where people can experience connection to God and community with others in the best way possible.

I'm happy that the church was expanded by its use of gymnasiums in the 1980s and '90s, but we lost something profound. We lost the sensuality of spirituality and replaced it with song after song in the key of C, metaphorically speaking. I love music, but we've underestimated the power of physical design. Environment is how we exist on the earth! Not my idea, but God's. You may not feel that you are "into design," but because we are humans created in God's image, design is wired into us.

Addressing engaging environments, Andy Stanley encourages church leaders to ask, "Is the setting appealing?" and challenges us not to discount the importance of paying close attention to aesthetics:

It could be argued that the very first thing God did in time was to create an appealing environment tailored for his prize creation, that portion of creation that would be fashioned in his image, the image of the one who created an irresistible environment. Essentially, that's the story of creation.(*Deep & Wide* [Grand Rapids: Zondervan, 2012], pp. 164–65)

Even as I write this, the absurdity of attempting to convince readers of God's creativity gene is beyond humorous: "In the beginning, God *created*." Bam. Forming the land, sky, plant and animal life, and subsequently human beings was the first recorded act of love that God chose to extend. Our call as humans and Christians—as "little Christs"—is to carry on the legacy, to not allow our busy, linear, routine-driven little lives to edge out the open, expansive, imaginative, and soul-tending nature of God, and to share that beautiful, authentic, holy "spirit" with a weary world.

Chapter 2

JESUS ON HOSPITALITY

My Father's house has room to spare. If that weren't the case, would I have told you that I'm going to prepare a place for you? When I go to prepare a place for you, I will return and take you to be with me so that where I am you will be too.

—*John 14:2-3*

Isn't it true that we measure our lives not in terms of numbers of days but in treasured, memorable experiences? During his time on earth, Jesus understood that it cost nearly nothing to take an everyday event and turn it into an incredible experience. This uncanny knack for engaging people in everyday settings demonstrated various themes on a wide variety of occasions. Consider these hosted galas:

- Jesus Christ Wedding Crasher: when Jesus made that humble-but-flashy first appearance, coming up with the finest wine of all at the wedding in Cana

- Jesus Catering Co.: when Jesus provided fish and chips to spare on the Galilean hillside

- Jesus the Upper Room Event Planner: even in his moments of greatest stress, Jesus outlined the menu, served the wine, and initiated the conversation

- Heaven's Kitchen on the Beach, starring Jesus as Master Chef: Jesus served fish tacos for the hungriest of disbelievers

On any of these occasions Jesus could have simply arranged a boardroom-style meeting room, requesting three tables to be arranged in a U-shape in a room boasting only blank whiteboards and outlets for laptops. Strangely, we see the God of all creation insisting that food and drink be the central magnetic force, pulling in the guests, providing the perfect natural resources to generate open, honest communication. People aren't looking for meetings. People are longing for meaning, and the care for physical bodies coupled with the nourishment of spiritual hope is a winning combination any day of the week.

Ginghamsburg is so committed to offering "radical hospitality" that—despite our mission-minded budget—we've allowed for a full-time staff director of hospitality and events. This person passionately recruits servants to greet, usher, direct parking lot traffic, staff our Welcome Center, and serve as medics and security personnel. Whatever needs your current church community might have, assuring that each guest feels welcomed and accommodated is imperative to a healthy, growing faith community.

It's important to assign someone who's fairly observant to periodically enter your campus and buildings with "fresh eyes," eyes that haven't traveled those parts a hundred times before. You'll want to assure that the spaces are clean, accommodating, and free of that "church garage sale" style, smell, and atmosphere. Although friendly greeters and clean pews are important, there may be some details of guest experience that we've not yet considered:

new guest and single-parent parking, outside greeters, strategically posted signage, and a clearly marked entrance are all extremely important to new seekers.

Inside the building, details such as a comfortable temperature setting, accessible water and refreshments, engaging children's spaces, and clearly identified directions will create the kind of experience most likely to keep guests returning. Of course, the ability to share a spirit of Christlike love is the most profound welcoming tool we possess.

As passionate as I am about the physical aspect of space design, I understand that the tastefully arranged spaces simply support the overriding goal of offering an impressionable, personable experience. Servant teams invested and empowered to carry out this "process of experience" will ensure that you've made a profound impression from the very first visit.

Preparing Places

A spirit of hospitality ran deep in Jesus' veins. We see it in his actions toward children, in his habit of sitting down to eat with his friends as a form of connection and community, and in the promise he made to the disciples as they worried over the possibility of their future without him: "I'm going to prepare a place for you" (John 14:3). Jesus knew that we function best in spaces prepared for hospitality.

Church work is a lot about preparation. We plan and prepare; God shows up and orchestrates the outcomes. Careful preparation is a godly act. I believe Jesus is still in the business of preparing places for people on earth, but it's through servants who understand the importance of hospitality—the art and theology of sacred space. Historically, the church has gathered in homes, cathedrals, church buildings, community centers, and school gymnasiums. There is no space that is more "spiritually correct" than others. Further inside this book we'll explore great possibilities for redesigning the buildings God has given us, transforming them into welcoming oases for seekers to experience God and to connect to a community.

Thankfully, worshiping communities inhabiting even the most traditional-looking churches are discovering new ways to use "old" space. Whether it's removing some fixtures from the platform area, placing media screens in tasteful locations, or casting a glow in just the right location with the strategic placement of candles or the soft glow of ambient light, there truly is always a way to work around the challenges.

Getting out of our collective, boundary-edged box, we can take a worship space built in the 1800s and transform it into a media-friendly conference room in which the furniture is arranged to suit the occasion. We can turn a worn-out 1960s "parlor" from an inner-city United Methodist church into a trendy Welcome Center that offers coffee and corners for conversations. We can upcycle a windowless, pinkish-purple room in the storefront property of an economically challenged

community—add ambient light, simple stage design, and affordable seating—and discover a "makes-me-wanna-worship" kind of sanctuary. These are new ways to use old space for the purpose of welcoming people.

Our Master Designer empowers us to risk creating welcoming spaces in entryways, worship settings, classrooms, offices, and fellowship halls. As I gather and organize my ideas and materials for an event or room design, I instinctively ask myself these questions with a fairly simple, whole-to-part kind of approach:

- What is the overall *theme* or *metaphor* we've decided upon?

- What must the designated space *feel* like (casual, friendly, traditional, urban, industrial, techno, country, natural, or modern)? There are dozens of "vibes" we could use as templates for our designs.

- What are the *colors* included in this series, season, or event? Sometimes the color scheme begins in a related sign or graphic advertising the event. Using related colors can create a sense of *branding*, which strengthens the outcome.

- What are the large objects, textures, metals, and styles we will use? Simplifying the options will unify the outcome. More on this later.

While I often work alone in the initial ideation/design process, I'm comfortable welcoming others into this step. When designing a space on one of our own Ginghamsburg campuses, I collaborate with the ministry leader who will most often use the space. I find great joy in asking what specific needs, hopes, and dreams are desired for the space and then pressing forward to fulfill those criteria in the best way possible. When our Tipp City lobby needed to be updated, I collaborated with our hospitality director as well as with some of our key leadership staff for this extremely important "main gate" space. We've undergone several transformations in fifteen years of building use; and for the first five years, we were convinced that we had no space for a real Welcome Center, but we were wrong. By pushing back a few walls, we literally transformed a coat closet into a full-blown Welcome Center. Modern furnishings and seasonally refreshed décor have created an engaging space for guests to receive a hearty welcome, a beautiful gift bag, and all the information one person could possibly desire. This "safe space connection

zone" serves as a community hub during busy campus events.

Recently we added warm pendant lighting along with tall bistro tables and stools to our main lobby. We realized that great community interaction could thrive only if we allowed space and time for it. We don't have the kind of large community entry space that many megachurches have, so we increased the time between worship celebrations to ease the crowding. Sometimes time and space can be interchangeable.

Mother's Day weekend is typically a big deal at Ginghamsburg. We see a surge in attendance because of infant dedications/baptisms, the children's choirs singing, and our annual Mother's Day flower sale hosted by one of our life groups (with all proceeds going to our Haiti mission). Our Ohio weather seldom cooperates in the early weeks of May, so we began staging this event in the main lobby. Each year I ask several of my "salvage sisters" to bring in some vintage garden pieces that will serve as staging platforms for

hundreds of plants. We set up two cash-and-carry stations, and—voilà—we have a beautiful, chaotic celebration of gifts for the moms we love.

Telling Your Story

People become what they see. New life pictures are vitally important to the discipleship process. That's why we at Ginghamsburg are careful not simply to say we want to be a multicultural community; we model racial diversity, age diversity, and gender diversity on our worship platforms and in our staff choices. In the same way, what we feature on our most visible wall spaces helps form who we are and shares the DNA of our church community with everyone who walks the hallways, from delivery persons to parents of preschoolers.

We created a wall to showcase our "Bring—Grow—Serve" mission statement using three photographs. We've designed several versions of the wall over the years, but our current look includes a solid, dark-colored wall paint, three framed photos carefully chosen and printed at an office supply store (for a higher quality than our in-house poster printer), a balanced layout using die-cut text letters, and a touch of added decals from a local home improvement store.

> BRING seeking people into a life celebration with Jesus
> GROW as disciples in cell community
> SERVE out of our call and giftedness

When consulting with churches who are ready to redesign their entry spaces, I've often suggested that they center their entryway walls around the one vision or mission they want to be about. Photographs speak volumes, and very few words are actually needed. For several years we designed entryway installations featuring large photographs of our mission in Sudan. We refreshed these displays yearly with beautiful colorful photos that richly depicted those positively affected by our investments in that war-torn country.

Recently I felt it was time for a change, so down came the photographs and up went the prayers. We connected this "prayer wall" to our Advent scripture and theme of good news from Isaiah 61:1:

> The LORD God's spirit is upon me,
>   because the LORD has anointed me.
> He has sent me
>   to bring good news to the poor,
>   to bind up the brokenhearted,
>   to proclaim release for captives,
>   and liberation for prisoners.

Reluctant to remove the backdrop drywall and wood installation, we treated the painted drywall with a stamped-paint application and lightly stained the large raw wood squares. Servants installed hundreds of screws, and we decoupaged printed scripture and the words *rebuild, restore,* and *renew* onto the drywall.

Manila tags were inserted into each

worship bulletin on the first weekend of Advent, and we invited worshipers to write their own prayer and drop it in the basket provided as they walked up to receive Communion. Following this, servants knotted and hung the tags, finishing out the wall. It's a beautiful, tactile, earthy kind of display of humans trusting God in expectation of our Christmas hope.

Whatever else is going on to attract and disciple the people of our world, offering the hospitality Jesus modeled must be at the top of the list. Time spent faithfully preparing spaces can seem costly, inconvenient, and downright difficult, but as the servants on our makeover team tell one another, "It's worth it!" It won't be long before you see signs of new life springing up out of old, tired places.

Chapter 3

A MINISTRY OF MUD 'N SPIT

Creativity can solve most any problem.
The creative act, the defeat of habit by originality
overrides everything.

—*George Luis*

What does it take to make a miracle happen?

In our own limited perspectives, we fancy God with sparkling magic potions carefully arranged in a glittering heavenly toolbox and maybe a few wands thrown in for the really tough jobs.

God's best work, however, has always been done with amazingly ordinary stuff—water, mud, spit, a piece of stale bread, a barn, a teenage girl, or twelve dysfunctional disciples—ordinary objects in regular places with everyday people. The good news for every single person on the planet is that miracles happen when the divine intersects with the ordinary.

I am but one woman with a very alternative education. I think way too many thoughts and have a passion for Jesus and the church. I'm not a very big person, and I still get knots in my stomach every time we embark on a new makeover project; but look out when I set my mind to something.

The metaphor I've named for my life is "mud 'n spit." I'm fascinated with the four Gospels and the earthiness of everything Jesus did. I'm not sure how Jesus would've healed the blind man in the Gospel of John in chapter 9 if the miracle had occurred in this millennium. Maybe he would've used some thick espresso or some aromatic

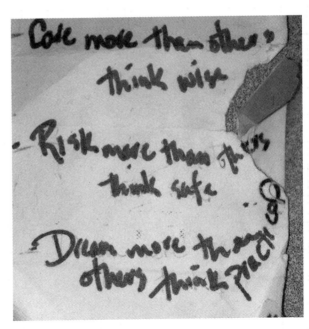

candle wax. On that particular day, however, Jesus spit in the dust, making a clay paste with his saliva, and he rubbed that paste onto the blind guy's eyes and then told the guy to go wash in a certain pool. That's creativity. That's using what you have, where you have it, and whom you have it with—I love that! Stories like that give me hope that I can do this, too. I'm an everyday person. I've been touched by heaven, empowered by God. I can use what God has already put in me and around me—just ordinary stuff—and begin to change the world one space at a time.

Ours is a ministry of mud 'n spit. God wants each and every one of us to know that with God's Spirit, we are uniquely gifted to be a part of making miracles happen. We are just everyday people using ordinary objects in regular places to create powerful God moments. And as we dive into makeover mania here, I would like to share a few words that I keep on a tattered yellow sticky note next to my computer:

- Care more than others think wise

- Risk more than others think safe

- Dream more than others think practical

- Expect more than others think possible

Design Mantras

Whether I take on a stage design, an office remodel, or a lobby makeover, it occurs to me that I tend to operate under a system of "design mantras" that guide the makeover process. These principles help give form to what can feel like an ominous and daunting task. Let's take a look at the key mantras I advise our team to follow again and again:

1. Less Is More

There's probably a reason this mantra has made its way to the top of the list. I can't count how many times I've walked inside a church building only to be smacked upside the head with massive, unrelated items stuffed in every corner and hallway, bare-legged folding tables sporting out-of-date brochures, bulletin boards featuring photos of people I've never seen in my life, nametags shouting "You're not part of our church!" and random food-collection baskets sitting on a too-small table fronted by a poorly hand-scrawled sign. It all starts to feel like a Sunday school version of *Hoarders*.

Good design is generally clean design. There must be a sense of order and purpose, for this is the stewardship God has entrusted to us. Practicing "less is more" is like editing a picture—deleting the clutter, the distraction, and those pieces that keep your eye wandering and "worried." There is great visual strength in eliminating what doesn't matter in the grand scheme of things in order to appreciate the beauty of what does matter. Design boards are helpful tools to clarify the color schemes, materials, and a general cohesive "vibe."

One of our very first design projects at Ginghamsburg involved transforming the meeting area of our original 1800s brick church building now named the ARK into a media-friendly conferencing room. We determined that we wanted to retain some of the old features of the room such as high ceilings, tall stained-glass windows, an archive of historic photos, and partially exposed wood flooring.

Our first priority was to create a design board with our chosen colors to incorporate lighting styles, countertop choices, and wood grain and color. Three designers collaborated on that project, but it was our design board that became the bad guy. If it didn't match what was on the board, we didn't choose it or use it. Gathering materials for any project becomes a lot more enjoyable when those first simplified choices help determine yea or nay. And the results of that room in the ARK are still amazing years later, largely because we chose complementary colors and key materials and stuck with our choices. *Less is more.*

Fast-forward several years and a second campus later. Our newly acquired Fort McKinley Church sported a basement so dingy it made me want to cry. We clarified a basic, fresh color scheme

to use throughout and defined a streamlined but quality environmental direction: metal wall pieces, drywall texture-treatment walls, black-brown dry-brushed paint on all paneled walls, and bamboo blinds on the windows. Being strict with our choices created a refreshed, updated feeling. Within six months, that basement was home to a full-blown food pantry, a used-clothing shopping corner, a professionally furnished classroom, and a large outreach office—all displaying a design sense that truly made us proud. *Less is more!*

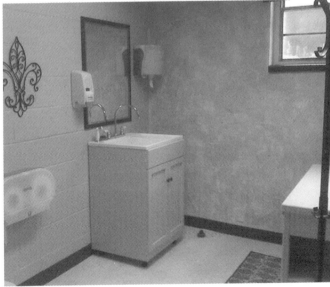

2. Embrace What You Cannot Change

I've learned a prayer from my friends in recovery. It's a prayer I say often. Perhaps you know it as well:

> God, grant me the serenity
> to accept the things I cannot change,
> the courage to change the things I can,
> and the wisdom to know the difference,
> Amen.

Truth be known, I say this prayer under my breath on a fairly regular basis. Time spent in worry and frustration over anything not in my power to change is really wasted time, and I can't stand the thought of wasting anything—much less my precious, limited time. Embracing what we cannot change goes beyond acceptance of a faulty design dilemma. To embrace means to make use of something—in this case, to seize it and use it as part of your design picture.

Back to the Fort McKinley basement. Every room on that floor housed pipes across the ceiling—lots and lots of pipes. Generally one would work to hide pipes, but as we were painting that underground classroom, we decided that rather than attempt to hide the pipes—cutting off already limited height in the room—we would treat them as a design element and paint the entire menagerie of ceiling pipes our accent color (black-brown).

This created a much-improved open feeling in those rooms with low ceilings and gave the space increased visual interest. Jesus said his strength

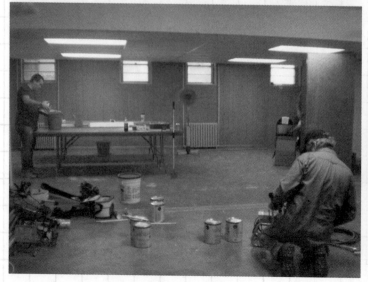

would be made perfect in our weakness. Isn't this basically the same principle at work? Embrace what you cannot change.

This past summer, as we set out to completely remodel our Ginghamsburg Kids ministry spaces, we discovered a large closet that could feasibly be knocked out and transformed into the "Starting Point" sign-in station. There was only one problem with this idea, and that was the huge I-beam standing smack-dab in the middle of this ideal location. Not easily daunted, I suggested we "embrace" the I-beam in the center of the room and transform it into a tree. At the time I had no experience in tree making and absolutely no idea how we would go about

creating a 3-D tree. I believe, however, that saying the plan out loud gives it credibility and accountability and activates our faith in what God can do. This time God would have to fill in what I didn't know. Can you say "clueless"?

Embracing the I-beam—and the idea of the tree—I began a Google search for handmade-tree plans, materials used for similar projects, and retail fake trees, just to get a visual (crazy expensive, by the way). In the end the only tutorials available required the use of toxic adhesives, which is a major no-no for our kids' and preschool area. Trusting past our ignorance, we covered the steel beam with a quarter-inch layer of plywood on all four sides. Next we wrapped the "trunk" with several yards of chicken wire, with the goal of changing a square post into a roundish trunk.

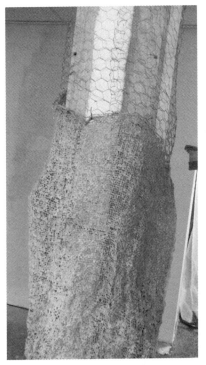

We used a moldable papier-mâché medium to form the roots on the floor and let that dry for twenty-four hours. Meanwhile, we searched for a similar medium suitable for our tree trunk. Feeling rather desperate, my fellow mud-'n-spit mate Lori Meyer grabbed an armful of landscape burlap (the

brown loose-weave fabric purchased in the landscape department of a home improvement store), since we always have yards of it around. Her thought was to cut it into strips, drag it through glue "decoupage" water, and then wrap the tree. Before we began wrapping, I decided to try taking that large length of burlap and suspending it from the top of the beam, allowing the fabric to hang vertically and creating generous folds that surprisingly gave us the authenticity of bark ridges on a tree. Who knew?

Once all the burlap was soaked in glue water, hung, and dried, we repeated the process to make five branches, each with a cardboard tube core wrapped in chicken wire and then wrapped again in glue-soaked landscape burlap (I did this part in my living room). Attaching the branches once everything dried was definitely the toughest part of the process, but we wired them in place using sheer force of will atop ladders of challenge. We attached the branches to the tree as best we could, also suspending them from the ceiling tiles using thin wire. We were careful to hang the branches high enough to avoid active children testing their climbing skills.

With the addition of leaves, our tree looks amazingly authentic. It's surprising what we are capable of when the only thing greater than our anxiety is the awareness that "no" is not an option. Next time you encounter what emerges as an obstacle, dare to *embrace what you cannot change.*

3. Discover Beauty on a Budget

One of my fondest memories from my teenage years is browsing through J.C. Penney's clothing department with my mom and sisters. We really never purchased anything. With four daughters in the house, all clothing was handmade. We were just browsing the styles. The very best part of this memory is of my mom's voice wafting over my shoulder, "Oh, you could make that, honey, so much prettier and for so much less." Of course, at the time I felt it was the curse of the parental, with the real translation being, "We cannot afford to buy you that, so you better get used to the idea that if you want something bad enough, you're going to have to make it yourself."

In the end it's not been such a horrible curse after all. Even now I seldom shop to purchase. I shop for ideas, and there's no limit or budget for ideas (just limited time for accomplishing all I see). My mom wasn't overly crafty, but she did equip me with a sewing machine, permission to experiment, and a boatload of encouragement.

Once when money was fairly tight, my younger sister, Tamie, and I badly wanted blazers we'd seen in a shop, but we didn't have the fabric to make them ourselves. Not to be discouraged, we dug copious fabric scraps out of the box in the pantry, cut them into squares, sewed all the squares together, and then cut our blazers out of this piecemeal yardage. We got our blazers after all. Of course, that was before patchwork was cool.

The point is, I never really consider lack of money as an obstacle. I know that my media-savvy coworkers absolutely must pay real cash for the newest items on their wish lists, but I have the luxury of a do-it-yourself mind-set. Rather than embark on a makeover project by thinking about how much this is going to cost us, I find myself fully focusing on how we can do the project before us for as little cash—and with as much class—as possible.

Being part of a missional church means that our "amazing space" financial priorities will be directed first toward those most in need, heavily toward the ministries of our own church family, and less toward the padded desires of our paid staff. That being said, our makeover team enjoys customizing Ginghamsburg's office spaces into cozy havens of meaningful productivity for staff persons who have joined the Ginghamsburg team. Aside from a small budget we have for wall paint, we set out to discover beauty on a budget. Check out this office makeover designed by one of our makeover-team servants, Madison Freeman:

The makeover team had the challenge of turning a small, dated storage room in our Fort McKinley building—complete with stained-glass windows—into a modern, contemporary office for a young, stylish music director. Unfortunately, modern, contemporary, and stylish can often mean spending a lot

of money unless you're willing to get creative. By embracing details about the space that we couldn't change and putting our heads together to figure out how to get the most bang for our buck, we achieved our goal without going over budget. Instead of splurging on artwork, we let painter's tape outline a funky stenciled wall treatment, and rather than spending a lot on custom organizational systems, we bought inexpensive hooks and boxes that filled the same need. Other materials such as donated milk crates, spray paint, and IKEA scratch-and-dent countertops allowed us to achieve a stylized, one-of-a-kind look that met all of our goals. Now our teaching pastor wants the same style of office!

Beauty on a budget—it's downright contagious!

Our Tipp City campus is the largest of Ginghamsburg's four Dayton-area locations and the flagship headquarters where our unique DNA must be incarnated. It's important to us to preserve a main lobby wall as a full-sized reminder of who we are and who we want to be. We set out to artistically visualize Ginghamsburg's threefold mission statement (Bring—Grow—Serve) in such a way as to be aesthetically pleasing while exercising financial restraint. We painted the entire wall a beautiful shade of green (green things grow, right?). And perhaps this would be a great time to acknowledge that the right color of paint and the wrong color of paint will cost you the exact same amount of money. In fact, the wrong color will cost you more after you've covered it with the right color; so if you need a consultant, hire one.

We then commissioned one of our servants with the task of creating the full text of the mission statement on her die-cut letter machine at home (free, because this is how she serves). Meanwhile, I set out to find three compelling in-house photographs (close-ups are good for this type of application) that each depicted one of the three parts of our statement and had them professionally printed at Staples. We did purchase frames from IKEA, which were all the same black-brown wood finish as the other accessory furnishings in our lobby areas.

The rest of this project involved the careful arrangement of photos and text and the finishing touches of a scaled-back decal application purchased from our local Menard. Total cost of this project came in at $120, but the ongoing message of the wall for all who grace its pathway is indeed priceless. *Beauty on a budget.*

4. Acquire the Unusual without Opening the Wallet

Our student activity center is a building that includes a large gymnasium, a large stage area, and several surrounding classrooms. In addition, a second-floor loft overlooking the gym hosts a hub of student activity, with a climbing wall, pool and Ping-Pong tables, a drink bar, and a small stage area. When the loft was ripe for a makeover several years ago, we painted the walls and added student-friendly design features to the various spaces of the room, but we seriously wanted to replace the ugly folding chairs and what I call "church tables." We had no budget for this unusual dream, however.

At the same time, a chef from our church family was building a brand-new restaurant in downtown Tipp City and had discovered a Dayton source for booths to install in his classy new space. Upon inquiry, we were awarded all the booths he could not use, free of charge! Makeover teammates managed all the transporting details that snowy January day, and I supplied reinforcements (a bit of paint, a roll of duct tape, and a large pot of chili). Several hours and a lot of elbow grease later, we'd retaped, repainted, and rearranged our way into a rather awesome student-ministry hangout space. We'd *acquired the unusual without opening the wallet,* yielding minimal cost and maximum results.

Our Tipp City campus has a southern portion a mile down South County Road 25A (we are soooo country!) that is home to our original building, which we call the ARK, as well as to the Discipleship Center, which housed our congregation from

1984 to 1994. The larger "worship area" of the Discipleship Center is now used for dinners, weddings, and funerals, and most days it is a hospitality room/food pantry where hundreds of guests seek assistance from our New Path outreach ministry all week long. The stage in that room is a platform typical of worship rooms built in the '80s—simple and functional. When asked to make the room media-friendly, we also were determined to put some design features around the stage to frame out the screen. At the same time, a Tipp City bank was being remodeled and had removed their wood railings, and I inquired about the possibility of using them at Ginghamsburg, hoping we could *acquire the unusual without opening the wallet.* My vision was to secure a section of the railing horizontally along the back of the stage and under the lowered screen and then to use the rest in a vertical fashion, hinged and flanking the screen on either side. This configuration helped "anchor"

the screen and gave credibility to the stage place-ment. Free railings plus four purchased hinges plus $20 worth of black canvas to line the back of the railings gave us a professional small-stage look for less than $50 (see photo below).

One of the most beautiful budget-friendly designs was our 2009 Advent large-stage set. We wanted to create a stunning Christmas-like display using nontraditional church elements, infusing the feeling of an outdoorsy win-

ter. I connected with one of our makeover servants whose forte is her gathering skill. What she doesn't already have, she knows where to find. This time I asked my salvage sister for twelve large, bare deciduous trees out of her ten acres of woods, which she delivered in her pickup truck. Meanwhile, another servant painted simple tree silhouettes onto long pieces of donated canvas fabric that we planned to mount directly onto the back stage walls— behind the real trees that were bolted to the back of the stage, eighteen inches out from the walls. The combination of these two mediums was stunning, a seemingly deep and beautiful tree line across the span of the large stage.

I commissioned another servant to create an Advent candle "sculpture" out of logs and candles gleaned from a recently closed florist shop. Another servant built a modest speaking podium using a slim tree trunk and a slab of smooth wood across the top. We added several freestanding streetlamps at the back of the stage as accents. Total cost for

hardware, a small can of paint, and some powdery snow for a special Christmas Eve effect was less than $100. Thousands of people enjoyed that incredible, organic design, and for the most part, *we acquired the unusual without opening the wallet.* Years later, people still tell me how much they loved that particular Advent environment.

5. Always and Never

Recently, while I was sharing consult notes with another church's team, it occurred to me that after I went home, they could potentially be frustrated. If notes fall out of their folders, they might try desperately to remember all the small changes I'd suggested. It occurred to me that a list of "always and never" reminders could actually be a gift to their process. They jumped at the chance to have a ruler by which to measure their steps. Here are some of the line items on that ruler:

- Always use fresh flowers and plant life. Nothing artificial, plastic, or silk.

- Use unscented candles freely only if and where they can be readily attended. No unlit candles in public places; they say, "We're not home!"

- Keep fabric window treatments to a minimum. Shades, shutters, blinds, or bare windows all present a clean, more professional look.

- Bulletin boards are extremely hard to keep current and are ineffective forms of communication in our digital age. Replace them with mission-statement walls or enlarged, framed photographs of your church's mission, servant activity, or other inspiring images.

- In public hallways and spaces, remove anything that does not pertain to the majority of your people and new guests.

- Soft, ambient lighting is always preferable to harsh, overhead fluorescent lighting.

- Clean carpets, windows, and restrooms speak volumes.

- Empower one trusted person (who possesses a sense of style) to oversee public areas to ensure a clutter-free, guest-friendly, and aesthetically pleasing environment.

- Determine space "owners" of any trouble spots that require a more thorough cleanout, and empower them to do whatever it takes. The freed-up space you'll gain is worth much more than any outdated book or dusty candle.

- Put a moratorium on random pieces of paper taped to walls and doors in public places. Important messages can be nicely framed.

In the end, redesigning spaces is a mission that's not about money. It's about creativity, using what you have where you have it, and who's standing close by, ready to pitch in and be part of the miracle. Don't get hung up on what you can't do; rather, figure out what's possible and go for it.

I don't know what projects loom in front of you, what challenge you are facing, or what kind of situation might be currently keeping you in a state of "stuck"; but sooner or later, you'll need to realize that less really is more. Embracing what you cannot change will un-jam the logs and make room for discovering beauty on a budget. You'll get an idea for acquiring the unusual without opening the wallet and make the money people very, very happy. I'm excited that you'll be joining me in a ministry of mud 'n spit.

PART 11

MAKEOVER MOMENTUM: THE WHO, WHAT, AND HOW OF NINE MAKEOVER PROJECTS

They will rebuild the ancient ruins;
they will restore formerly deserted places;
they will renew ruined cities,
places deserted in generations past.

—Isaiah 61:4

Perhaps you have an idea or an actual plan for changing the look of a room or a stage or an office. What now? How do you move forward and keep moving forward in the world of makeover mania?

The chapters in part II all describe a process I use over and over again. For both small projects and large, the process is the same—just scaled up or down according to the scope of the work. As you read through these pages, be sure to think about how you could translate the steps to customize the process for your own setting.

C h a p t e r   4

IGNITE YOUR COMMUNITY

If your actions inspire others to dream more, learn more, do more and become more, you are a leader.

—*John Quincy Adams*

The ongoing nature of the mission of Jesus—any part of the mission—reminds us that if left to our own devices, we will certainly fail. Jesus never left a solo player in charge of anything but always commissioned groups of two, three, or twelve; and he himself was a part of the micro team we know as the Trinity. Each player on that team has a distinct function and position, a unique role to play; and each is equally important and vital to the overall presence and purpose of God in our lives today.

There is power in the convergence of *team*. Just as powerful worship events require a great worship design team, engaging stage sets require a great design team. The good news is that there are men and women of all ages in your congregation who will find their own sweet spot of service among paint cans, ladders, and power tools. Your job is to lift the vision, call them into service, and support them throughout a successful venture.

Most of the years I served as Ginghamsburg's worship-design team leader we were a lean, mean, paid, staff-driven team made up of media and music ministry specialists, speaking pastors, and myself—a writer, producer, and promoter. When I segued into the new world of campus design, I was still employed by Ginghamsburg but knew I would need to carry out absolutely all our campus design projects without the benefit of any other paid personnel. This was a bit daunting, yet deep in my heart I was confident that surely there were many men and women of all ages who would enjoy putting their design and building skills to use for a significant cause. My task was simply to find them and paint a picture (pardon the pun) big enough to entice and connect these servants into helping the vision come to fruition.

I should explain that Ginghamsburg is a church with a strong DNA of service. We've embraced a mission statement with a simple strategy has been lived out day by day, week after week for more than thirty years: *Bring* others into a life celebration with Jesus, *grow* as disciples in cell community, and *serve* out of our call and giftedness (remember the mission statement wall in chapter 2?). Ginghamsburg has a long history of great teaching coupled with the awareness and practice of what it means to be servants. We don't identify ourselves as volunteers, for that is the language of a club or committee whose members believe they can work or not work based on personal preferences. Calling ourselves "servants" reminds us of our commitment into a new order, the kingdom of God, in which we take seriously the command to "present your bodies as a living sacrifice that is holy and pleasing to God. This is your appropriate priestly service" (Romans 12:1).

Serving is how we show our love for God. The only question is, *how* will we serve? Gratefully, the possibilities are endless, and painting, nailing, hanging, gluing, sewing, drywalling, and styling are all legitimate means of serving Jesus. It all matters. We understand that we are building environments in which seekers can come into faith. We are redesigning spaces for connection and community. Recruiting a team in this servant-mentality environment put me in a good position.

One of my first recruiting tools was a well-designed postcard-sized invitation I put together. Following is a snapshot of that postcard. I displayed the card at a ministry fair that our church hosted and also placed a few in our Welcome Center. Each time someone would respond—by either phone or e-mail—I asked what that person enjoyed doing and what kind of experience he or she might have. I've found that one of the keys to building a great team is making sure everyone gets to do a lot of what they like to do best. I enjoy partnering to figure out what that is for each person.

Soon I was tasked with the complete remodeling of the Fort McKinley campus. We acquired the building at the same time I was growing my own makeover wings. I put out an all-call in our church bulletin one weekend and personally contacted all who responded. We arranged to share a simple lunch and enjoyed a wonderful day painting the new Welcome Center and two hallways. I networked to determine who out of that group might want to hang in there and be part of the ongoing team, taking names and numbers. The next time we worked together I did the same thing. Pretty soon we were growing a fine core of servants with varying degrees of skill. At the same time, the bottom was falling out of our Miami Valley economy, and Ginghamsburg wisely hosted a class to encourage and advise those who had recently lost their jobs. I obtained a list of the students in that class and kept several of them very, very busy for about two months. We all rejoiced when one by one Jim, Seth, Patrick,

a call to ~ artist–builders ~

do you have a flair for the fabulous? is your secret dream to be part of the extreme home makeover team?

it's time to put yourself out there!

join the ginghamsburg makeover team, a group of artist-builders whose passion is to minimize brick, maximize mission and *mesmerize* the masses with the creative use of all our campus spaces... stages ~ classrooms ~ events! so, whether you're a builder, a painter or a candlestick-maker, chances are your talent is destined to help grow our ginghamsburg God-spaces.

email Kim @ kmiller@ginghamsburg.org and let us know what you love to do!

www.redesigningworship.org

Campus Design Team

ginghamsburg
Changing the World
...one life at a time

6759 South County Rd 25A
Tipp City, Ohio 45371
937.667.1069
ginghamsburg.org

Connect with the Ginghamsburg Church community online at www.facebook.com/ginghamsburg and www.twitter.com/ginghamsburg

and Tim each found a new place of gainful employment, but I can't help but marvel when I think back to how the Fort was transformed by servants who, when the going got tough, still got up and got going. As faith would have it, we designed new spaces and found connection and community in one another.

It's amazing to me how we always seem to have the right people on each project. My job is to cast vision, to recruit, and to connect. God's job is to get the right people for the task on any given day. I try not to freak out too much about the "right people" part. I'm learning that God's got this.

Casting vision is such an incredibly important piece of the team-building pie. Seth Godin's book *Tribes: We Need You to Lead Us,* contains more than a few noteworthy quotes on this topic of team leading. One of my favorites is: "The secret of leadership is simple: Do what you believe in. Paint a picture of the future. Go there. People will follow" ([New York: Portfolio, 2008], p. 108).

Sometimes I think my only real gift is that I can see things that haven't happened yet. My compulsion to propel those "dreams" to fruition is quite strong, and I do enjoy bringing others along into the process.

Since that first building season a few years ago, I've enjoyed working with a steady team of more than fifty makeover servants and several hundred one-time project servants when the call went out for special missional needs. Our makeover team has the reputation of creative, quality work, and each of our ministry areas now knows who to call on for any redesigning needs that might arise.

Along with each and every makeover project, new stage design, and event-styling gig, there must be a servant-recruitment step. This is done in the form of an e-mail sent at least two weeks ahead of time when possible. In our demographic, that's about the right amount of time to get the best response. When I write those e-mails, I ask that the team respond to me ASAP, letting me know when they are available during the hours given. When possible, I allow for daytime and evening work-hour options to include the wide variety of schedules people are juggling and then plan the work accordingly. This is a sample e-mail invite from a large build-out project we did early on:

Dear Friends and Fellow Servants,

I hope this finds you all well and enjoying the new year and all it holds. I have really missed working with the makeover team as some of my staff responsibilities have shifted in the last six months, but that brings me to the purpose of this e-mail.

We have an exciting opportunity coming up in the Avenue. After ten years of a relatively blank and uninviting stage in the large gym area, we recently received funds designated to build out the Avenue stage, creating a more engaging and visually rich location for student worship, activities, and large-group gatherings. I recently met with the Student and Children's Ministry team leaders and inputted their wishes into a design that will effectively serve both ministries in a regular and ongoing way. It's exciting to be part of moving these groups forward as they engage our children and grandchildren into faith.

This Avenue stage project will require significant carpentry skills (power tools—woo hoo!) and painting skills, both wall and artistic painting. There will undoubtedly also be a need for adaptable servants to help wherever needed as well—running to Menards, assisting workers, etc. Two servants have agreed to head up the carpentry parts of the project. **Project dates are Saturday, Feb. 6 and Saturday, Feb. 13 from 12:30 p.m. to 9:00 p.m.** We will work in the Avenue gym and backstage areas.

Because of the scope and importance of this project, I need to ask if you could e-mail me back the time(s) you are able to serve so that we can arrange the project accordingly. Once we know the team and times available, we can arrange the schedule and e-mail back to you more details about what to bring and what you should be prepared to do.

God's blessings to all of you. I'm looking forward to reconnecting! Should you be unable to help this time around, please e-mail me to let me know how you're doing these days.

Kim

On project day it's always golden when veteran servants show up who can take simple instructions and zoom forward without a lot of detailed instruction. I always know who my newest servants are and must keep in mind that they will require extra training time. I'm definitely not the world's greatest administrator and still work hard to maximize every moment of every servant's time. We are always doing new things—inventing and experimenting along the way. So leading a design team of any sort is definitely not a calling for the faint of heart.

Teamwork is at its best when the servants connect with one another and multiply the training opportunities. I like to partner a new servant with a veteran if it looks like they can successfully work on a task in tandem.

My favorite moments are when we gather to embark on a project and see servants who are genuinely excited to reconnect again. This grace-filled connection and community turns our ordinary projects into extraordinary God experiences. What a great feeling! But don't just take it from me; check out what some of the makeover-team servants had to say about their own experiences serving on the makeover design team.

Chad

I became part of the makeover design team at the conclusion of my Ministry by Strengths course at Ginghamsburg. I remember my table leader saying that my graphic arts interests and [Gallup StrengthsFinder] Strengths of Input, Adaptability, and Relator made me a good fit for this team. My first "major league" project involved turning green construction paper, florist wire, and volleyball poles into seven-foot palm trees for our Good Friday "Journey to the Cross." Those trees took me the entire day, and they came out absolutely terrible. I was genuinely heartbroken that my big break in creative servitude was a strikeout and was sure that I'd be sent back down to the minors. Imagine my surprise when everyone said the palm trees looked great and I was invited to serve on many other design projects.

I attend worship, serve on mission trips, and was part of the life-group community, but all those things pale in comparison to the raw connection I feel to God's purpose for me when I spend a day building set props or décor items. Like most people, my day job is hectic and stressful, and each day usually ends with me feeling two feet tall and knowing there's another one just like it tomorrow. The funniest part about being on a design project is knowing that it will be every bit as hectic and stressful but that I always feel ten feet tall when it's done. Every time. That is the power of God working in me, through my passions and my hands to affect others, and I am so very grateful.

Erin

I took the Ministry by Strengths class offered at Ginghamsburg and learned that we can serve best by using the interests and gifts given to us by God. To me, aesthetics have always been so obviously important to the success of any presentation. I believe this is true even when it's not obvious to a person. I love that the work our team does operates on a stealthy, subconscious, almost magical level, to help worshipers feel the presence of the Holy Spirit. . . .

Serving on the team has also helped me see that we can serve as helpers and followers in areas that correspond to our natural interests and that we can serve as catalysts and leaders in areas that we are passionate about and called to. Serving on the design team, I'm frequently amazed at what God is able to do through someone he's given his vision to and with the help of others. In the CSA garden ministry I lead, I can see this same dynamic at work as I inspire servants to help me achieve a vision from God.

Jen

I joined the design team after many God nudges. I had been attending Ginghamsburg for several years, but I wasn't yet serving or connected in any other significant way. I sneaked into the back of the worship area and left often without being noticed. I kept admiring the work that the makeover team was doing and kept hearing Kim ask for new servants to join the team. It was an invitation from a friend to help out at a makeover and her assurance of how non-threatening the work was that got me to finally stick a toe in the water. I haven't been the same since.

Once I began serving with the Design Team, God began growing a gift of creativity in me past anything that I would have thought myself capable of. I've realized so much about the talents that I've been given and have found so much joy in putting them to good use to glorify God. New creative projects and redesign inspirations have extended from Ginghamsburg to my office and home space. What a blessing it's been to be opened up to the work that God is doing in me.

Lori

Our family first attended Ginghamsburg Church over a decade ago. We found the message challenging, the music uplifting, and the surroundings stimulating. Each Sunday, being a visual person, I would look around and wonder, "Who created this? How did they do it?" I secretly imagined painting a backdrop or helping with a project, although I didn't know who to contact or how to help. One Sunday I saw an invitation in the bulletin for anyone interested in taking part as a design-team member, and I answered the call. It was love at first brushstroke, and I've been involved ever since.

The advantage of being a member of a larger congregation is that there are so many opportunities to help and so many people ready to answer the call. Therefore, it's more feasible to serve out of your strengths. In the past I had worn the hats of Sunday school and Bible school teacher, Christmas play director, church council member, coordinator of our (at the time) church's booth at a local festival, and even church secretary; but I can honestly say that I feel most fulfilled serving when I am creating, cutting, painting, or sewing for a design-team project!

Madison

I became part of the makeover design team when I moved to Ohio in the fall of 2009. I was new to the area and to Ginghamsburg, jobless, and in need of a way to connect with others and fill up my time with purposeful activities. Someone connected me with the design team, and I fell in love. I had never had the opportunity to serve the Lord or my church community through my artistic gifts before. Upon landing a teaching job later that year, I struggled with giving up all the time I had been spending serving with the design team because I'd connected so well and loved it so much. Now, I still get to serve in small doses and enjoy every minute. Serving on the makeover design team fits me. I enjoy serving and the feeling of helping the Ginghamsburg community as well. It makes me feel like a "hand doing a hand's job."

Clark

I became part of the makeover design team when my I saw it was an opportunity to serve together with my wife (Kim) and use the skills God has given both of us. Ever since I was young, I have been involved in some sort of building project. Through high school and college, I built stage sets, and as an adult, I designed and built several homes. Working on the makeover team was an opportunity to take those skills and interests and use them for God's purpose, creating engaging environments for worship.

In addition, I get to work with great, fun people who also love to work hard and efficiently. Almost every project we take on brings a limited amount of time and a limited budget, a lot of creative ability, and a common goal toward an incredible design. It is exciting to see it all come together. At times, I have entered our worship area and felt amazed at how well our skills have come together to create a unique backdrop and to enhance the overall worship experience.

Jody

I became part of the makeover design team when I heard an announcement made that painters were needed for our newly acquired campus, the Point. I love painting and had seen a few other requests for painters but had been pregnant at the time or otherwise unable to help. This time I was free and excited to serve! Once I stepped up to serve, it opened up doors to other design serving opportunities as well.

I enjoy serving in this way because I learn new creative ideas and make great connections and friendships! I also love being a part of making the worship area—as well as other areas in the church buildings—exciting and beautiful for those who attend each week.

A special note from Kim: I love my team. We've worked, played, eaten, and even traveled to distant cities to work together on a mission. The makeover design team has become one of my closest life groups as we share *communitas*, which is best defined as an intense common spirit coupled with a goal of serving the greater community. On my days of greatest discouragement (and yes, they do come), I realize the gift of this team, and it pulls me forward to a place of gratefulness and hope for all God's best. And to quote Martha Stewart, that's a good thing.

Chapter 5

Express Your Creativity

Think left and think right and think low and think high.
Oh, the THINKS you can think up if only you try!

—*Dr. Seuss,* Oh, the Thinks You Can Think!

Being a missional church means much more than a clever branding statement on a fancy conference brochure. Theologically, it means we're taking Jesus' call to reach out to the least and lost quite seriously. Logistically, it's a strategy for decision making that permeates everything we do and how we spend our resources. "Minimize brick, maximize mission" has been our repeated phrase to keep us from resorting to new buildings as a solution to our space challenges. Rather, we strive to pack as much missional activity into as little space as possible, and those very same spaces must serve as many needs as possible on any given day. For instance, in the span of one typical week, our Tipp City worship center hosts six weekly worship celebrations, including one for clients of our food pantry (Gateway Worship) and one for people on the road to recovery (Next Step Worship). It's also a preschool playground every weekday, a large family-style dinner space, a Bible study venue, a staff chapel and meeting space, and a café environment for an evening vision-casting dinner. The place never cools off!

This challenge has caused us to become quite creative and resourceful in terms of discovering new ways to use "old" space. Whether it's removing some fixtures from the platform area, adding café tables, placing media screens in tasteful locations, or casting a glow in just the right location with the strategic placement of candles or ambient light, there truly are dozens of ways to work around our greatest challenges. Let's take a tour of some of our most contagious community spaces.

Ginghamsburg Kids Spaces

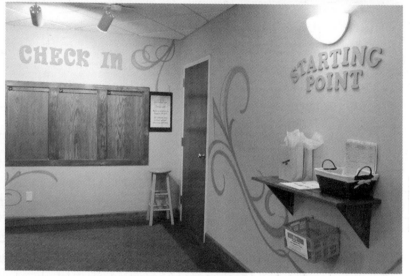

Recently, upon realizing our children's spaces were in desperate need of rebranding and reimagining, Ginghamsburg Kids director Erica Sharp coordinated a massive one-month makeover. Here's her description of what took place:

When we began to refocus on our children's ministry this past fall, one of the first places we started was our Ginghamsburg Kids space. We started with our ten-year-old design: wall-to-wall nature murals, bulletin boards, and posters advertising events. The murals were beautiful, but as we unpacked who we wanted to be as a ministry, we quickly realized our space needed to clearly tell our story. We couldn't assume simply providing awesome discipleship opportunities would engage our kids. Our goal was that our families would know exactly what our purpose was from the moment they set foot in our space.

We began by creating a family drop-off and parking zone so that even our parking lot would shout that kids are a priority at Ginghamsburg. In our preschool area, we focused on a kid-friendly color scheme to complement our curriculum, Orange (whatisorange.org), and simple, whimsical starbursts that dance across our walls, leading from room to room. Our three end goals—framed in bright, coordinating col-

REdesigning churches

A Closer Look

Check out these photos for more detailed information,
ideas, and instructions from projects included in this book.
Plus a bonus section of photos only included here!

Tips & Techniques

Fort McKinley Basement

SMALL LAMP

LIVE PLANT

CHEST-HIGH COUNTERTOP

A few simple touches convey warm hospitality; an old chest-high counter painted to match the space creates a guest-friendly information station. A live plant and a cheerful lamp offer an intimate corner. Resist the urge to overdo—less is more!

WARM PAINT COLORS

Notice the iron scrollwork cross-wall décor repeated throughout the Fort McKinley building. The background wall is actually cement block covered with drywall joint compound—spread with a spackling knife, sculpted, and color-washed to create a warm, old-world look. The warm color scheme is consistent throughout the public spaces of the building—keeping the costs down and the classiness up!

IRON SCROLLWORK CROSS

Ginghamsburg Kids Starting Point & Check In

WOOD LETTERS

DESIGN MOTIF

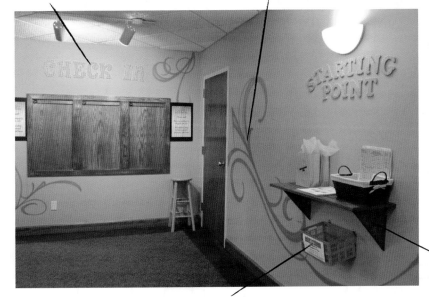

Branding spaces for age groups or ministry areas is great design fun and helpful for guest recognition. Vibrant color schemes, consistent font letters (purchased and painted) and skillfully painted wall design all provide interest and engagement. Track lighting, bracketed shelves, and labeled organizing baskets contribute to a sense of calm and thoughtful preparation.

WOOD SHELVES

ORGANIZING BASKETS

HALLWAY BANNERS AND POSTERS

Ginghamsburg Kids Hallway

FAUX FENCING

Mission statements become wall art that reinforces faith and purpose for kids and parents alike. Faux fencing was created by applying slats of wood-look laminate flooring vertically. Individual adhesive-backed pieces were cut, dog-eared at the top and spaced an inch apart. A cost-friendly way to customize a space.

Notice the large room number above the door. Purchased and painted numbers are easy to hang and make room recognition a breeze for new guests while keeping the environment fun for the kids!

LARGE ROOM NUMBERS

CHEERFUL PAINTED GEARS

FAUX BRICK

Once again, a few repeated elements and a consistent color scheme can go a long, long way toward creating a vibrant albeit professional look.

Pop-Up Bookstore

SCROLLWORK
METAL EASELS

BLACK SHELVES

POTTED
PLANT

LIBRARY
CHAIR

No room for a bookstore? Notice how this pop-up bookstore is staged right IN the back of the worship center for the occasion of a conference. Consistent furnishings such as the metal scrollwork easels, black-brown shelving units and burlap covered foam board are used over and over and over again in different ways for events, weekend worship, and occasional conferences. Intentionally placed displays help delineate the bookstore footprint.

Common Grounds Cafe

INEXPENSIVE
LIGHT FIXTURES

Low-cost light fixtures can create a stunning focal point in any room. Hung at different levels these "stained-glass" pendants blend coffee shop with church hardware. Repeat colors in other materials—walls, carpet, and furnishings. Use lamps to create warmth and add light, to perk up corners, and highlight conversation areas. It is not visible in this photo, but when possible, paint acoustic tiled ceilings black or brown to add warmth and ambiance to any room.

The Gathering Storefront

Notice the well-designed, creative, easy-to-read sign, the friendly potted plants, and the neat and clean entrance. A storefront church can be very inviting.

EASY-TO-READ SIGN

POTTED PLANTS

The Naz

STAINED GLASS WINDOWS

Beloved, old stained glass windows are hung in a new space. Find ways to use meaningful or significant elements from older buildings. Give old, traditional pieces new life by using them a new way in a new space and it's a visual win-win. What a great way to honor your congregation's heritage.

Take Time to Sketch It Out

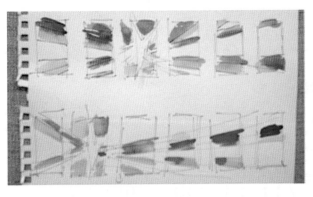

Sketch out your ideas in advance. Include the key elements scaled as well as possible. A perfectly detailed diagram is not as important as communicating key concepts with your teammates. They will greatly appreciate seeing the vision and be equipped to work harder once armed with that extra information.

Add heavy duty casters to platforms, stage flats, furnishings and other visual elements. Making pieces mobile will give you greater flexibility and allow use of elements creatively in different spaces.

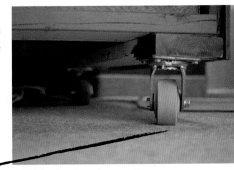

HEAVY DUTY WHEELS

FLOOR COVERINGS

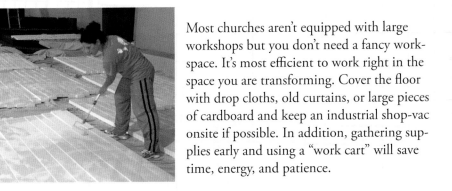

Most churches aren't equipped with large workshops but you don't need a fancy workspace. It's most efficient to work right in the space you are transforming. Cover the floor with drop cloths, old curtains, or large pieces of cardboard and keep an industrial shop-vac onsite if possible. In addition, gathering supplies early and using a "work cart" will save time, energy, and patience.

Worship Space ReDesign

Fort McKinley

Fort McKinley worship space: before.

PLATFORM EXTENSION

Servants building platform extension, bridging the gap between worship leaders and congregants.

IRON SCROLLWORK CROSS

The metal scrollwork, materials, and colors are repeated throughout the building. For example, iron open-work candle jars on windowsills, same paint on walls, and simple new window treatments—which allow light to come in, but add warmth and a sense of welcome.

The contemporary worship setup: A screen drops into place and ironwork crosses are removed and replaced with visual elements related to the sermon series or worship service; in this case, hand-painted statements/scripture passages on boards; ladder as "banner pole," pedestals as candle holders and pulpit, rug on platform. Simple walls, movable furnishings, and visual elements.

SERMON VISUAL ELEMENTS

PEDESTAL CANDLE HOLDERS

LADDER "BANNER POLE"

DECORATIVE RUG

IRON SCROLLWORK CROSSES

The traditional worship setup: Iron scrollwork crosses adorn the walls; altar, candleholders, organ all moved into place. Walls and raised pulpit have been removed, chancel now extends into congregation. No more "us and them." A simple padded stool is the worship leader seating. Simple, natural visual elements are in warm tones—scrollwork, wood candle pedestals, sheath of wheat. Warm, buttery color on walls, arch in contrasting warm brown, white ceiling, clean deep red carpet throughout. All of this highlights the historical church architecture and creates a warm, inviting, visually consistent, and pleasing environment.

TRADITIONAL WORSHIP INSTRUMENTS

TRADITIONAL ALTAR

Message Series Stage Design

The Holy Spirit

What are you trying to convey? That is a good first question to ask when brainstorming ideas for visual elements in worship. What words describe the sensations, feelings, or sights that you want to communicate? For the Holy Spirit series, we wanted to evoke a sense of movement. Words like sparkle, shine, and shimmer described what we wanted the congregation to see.

SMASHED ALUMINUM CANS

"What is in your hand?" is a great place to start. What is available out of your home, office, and even your recycling bin? Chances are you will come upon some material or items that will spark your creativity. Smashed aluminum cans shimmer and shine, especially when light is shining on them. And gold paint, applied from plastic condiment bottles, sparkles with lovely color.

ADHERE ELEMENTS
WITH NAILS, SCREWS
OR STAPLE GUN

CRUSHED
SODA CANS

WEED CLOTH
BACKDROP

BICYCLE
BASKET TIED
TO WAIST
HOLDS SMALL
SUPPLIES

Weed Cloth Backdrop (Weed cloth is sold in
rolls in landscaping departments)

GOLD PAINT APPLIED
IN THICK STREAKS

CRUSHED
SODA CANS

Find ways to pull your stage designs out into the room. This creates excitement for worship, continuity, and crowd engagement.

MY GOD'S NOT DEAD
HE'S SURELY ALIVE
HE'S LIVING ON
THE INSIDE
ROARING LIKE A LION

For this series we lit the back wall design and kept all other stage elements to a minimum. Less really is more and the shimmery, dynamic design was beautiful and stirring for our congregation throughout the series.

STAGE IS CLEAR
OF DISTRACTIONS

WORSHIP TEAM
CAN BE
UNDER-LIT

Special Bonus Photos

We created this series in the summer of 2013. It is an example of using low-cost or no-cost, readily-available materials to great effect.

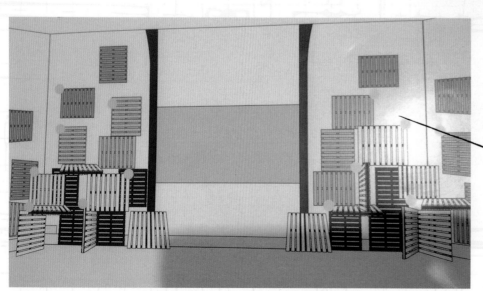

SERIES
DESIGN DRAWING

Use one material repeated in different ways to great impact. In this case the walls were not strong enough to support pallets so we built "faux pallets" out of foam cut to size and connected by lightweight wood slats.

FAUX PALLETS
MADE OF FOAM

PALLETS STACKED
VERTICALLY AND
HORIZONTALLY

Here, a local pallet vendor donated clean, new pallets.

THEATRICAL LIGHTING

STACKED PALLET DESIGN

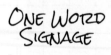

REBEL JESUS

ONE WORD SIGNAGE

We added one-word signage to communicate the key themes, and we added one pop of red/white color with the Renegade flag. Colored lighting changed the mood for different segments in the worship service, and added interest to the simple stacked pallet design. The visual effect was striking, and it was relatively straightforward for our servants to install with basic equipment.

One handmade stencil is used repeatedly across the stage on cloth and wood.

THEATRICAL LIGHTING

ors—clearly state our purpose to hallway guests and parents. In the midst of our four-week renovation frenzy, we incorporated an awkward I-beam into our plans and turned it into a tree! Check-in kiosks at every entrance serve to keep our kids accounted for and safe.

Our elementary kids' space features the same basic color scheme with intensified hues. A large hallway wall of graffiti art depicts our three end goals, specific to this age group, and we added segments of faux brick board to complete the urban look. We're excited about the "I Belong to Jesus" decision wall on which our kids stamp their handprints with paint and sign and date when they commit their lives to Jesus.

We also use music as another way to tell our story, using a reasonably priced sound system to play the same tunes in our hallways that our kids sing during their worship times. Other features are carpet squares—replaced easily when stains occur—and large, easy-to-read numbers that designate each room. Our Ginghamsburg Kids spaces now tell a story that is true to who we are and is completely consistent with the mission God has called our servant team and our families to accomplish together!

Avenue Gym

The walls in the large gym area of our student activity center, the Avenue, were a dated and scratched turquoise and peach—definitely not "guy" or athletic colors. I partnered with our men's ministry leader to coordinate the date, the materials, the lunch, and the one professional painter who ably led the troops. It was exciting to see forty twenty- to sixty-year-old men come early one Saturday morning and work side by side like they'd been painting together all their lives.

Five hours later, the guys were done! They loved the new colors, and I did, too. Cost of paint was about $500. Cost of labor was $0. End community result? Priceless.

Heritage Room @ the Fort

Our Fort McKinley campus church came to us complete with one hundred years of rich history—and hundreds of photos to prove it. We kept and repurposed the wood salvaged from the chancel area of the sanctuary as wainscoting for the Heritage Room. A new color scheme and vine/burnished metal lighting fixtures served to enhance the leaded glass windows, and we began to see the potential for a "wall of faith"—a creative display of carefully chosen photos from the Fort's rich

history. We purchased and painted twenty-four-inch squares of drywall and then printed sepia copies of all the photos chosen for the project.

Matching all the photos into the same sepia color scheme was the key to a cohesive look. We arranged them in chronological order onto eight drywall squares with room on the eighth square reserved for good things yet to come. The "bling" of the project was the use of small pieces of wood trim—some salvaged and some purchased pieces—painted to match the wood grain of the wainscoting, which added visual appeal to the overall display. Seeing the legacy of God's work is always cool—but better to feature in a less-public area.

A Mission-Inspired Classroom

Strange as it may seem, we have only one adult classroom in our entire main building at the Tipp City campus. This classroom, like our worship center, is used nearly every day of the week for a wide range of classes and events—with a different setup for each situation. The room had originally been designed for a future second floor, rendering its ceiling about eighteen feet high. Realizing that a second floor was not going to happen, we set out to create a more intimate venue, thus painting the ceiling and the top eight-foot portion of the walls completely black. We then suspended twenty-five pendant lights that created a faux ceiling feeling.

Wainscoting was installed on all four walls, and thirteen large framed posters of Ginghamsburg servants on mission were displayed on all four walls. Finally, we stenciled Matthew 25:40 around the periphery of the room just above the chair rail. It's impossible to sit in that room and not feel the power of the missional DNA we all share.

Prayer Rooms

Two of the first spaces I redesigned a few years ago were our prayer rooms at the Tipp City campus. I had recently toured United Theological Seminary and was inspired by their student-designed prayer room, furnished with unconventional rugs, lamps, floor pillows, candles, and soft seating. I learned that seminary students had requested a place for prayer and reflection and were given a closet and $500 to create this customized space.

Ginghamsburg, however, had two designated prayer rooms—sagging just a bit—and no "real" money to make significant changes. I went to work gathering up some items we had in our storage area: small rugs, bamboo sticks, and streetlamps (using low-watt flickering bulbs that stay on all the time). We added a shelf for a vial of oil, a prayer box, and a box of tissues. The goal of this space was to draw seekers in and provide the option to retreat to a tranquil space for conversation and prayer.

Is a designated prayer space important to your community? Do you have a closet, a small room, or extra space that could be repurposed into a prayer room for your church family? Try out your own creative skills, and feel the rewards of redesigning an out-of-the-ordinary space.

Bookstore Kiosk @ the Fort

At one of our acquired Fort McKinley campuses, we were asked to create a Ginghamsburg kiosk-style bookstore (aka "the Vine") that would be lockable and somewhat movable. The hope was to attract a bit of attention and enable the Fort to sell resources, message CDs and DVDs, and various Ginghamsburg mission T-shirts. I researched carts and found them online starting at around $1,000—a bit pricey. At the same time, we'd been remodeling a large classroom at the Fort where I'd noted a large cabinet standing empty.

We dry-brushed that piece of plywood furniture with a light coat of black-brown paint, and I was excited to repurpose that classroom cupboard into a bookstore kiosk! We installed new locks, moved the cupboard out into the worship lobby on casters, and stenciled a design onto the front. Paint plus mud 'n spit equals a beautiful bookstore location.

Music Office

When time allows, our team enjoys welcoming new staff with a customized office makeover. It's fun to listen to their personal stylistic wishes, think about what kind of resources are available at the time, and strategize the best use of the space allotted.

When our director of Worship and Music, James Keith Posey, arrived at Ginghamsburg, we offered him a fresh look for his long and windowless office space. He handed over a favorite painting, *Praying for Peace* by David Garrett, which features beautiful tones of orange

and green. While listening to JK, we made some notes about his wishes: orange was his favorite color, and he needed some wall shelves and hoped to have space for the band to hang out and play music on occasion.

We painted and stenciled two walls with a fun combination of green, rust, and brown, installed simple black shelving, and mounted a long mirror on the wall to widen the feeling of the narrow room. One of our salvage sisters provided a metal workbench that the team sanded and repainted metallic silver—very cool! The same sister offered a galvanized metal baseball backboard that we mounted on the wall to provide a backdrop for the many crosses in JK's personal collection.

JK added an orange couch and a black chair from home, and I must say that office has never looked better. The room now feels fun, warm, and inviting, and I'm pretty sure JK agrees.

Baptism on the Lawn

Several years ago, our pastor, Mike Slaughter, returned from a conference held at a church in Hawaii, where they apparently baptized a hundred or more new converts in the Pacific Ocean at the close of the conference worship. Of course, Mike—being Mike—returned to the cornfields of Ohio with the great idea to replicate that experience on the grassy front lawn of Ginghamsburg.

"No problem, Mike. Never mind that our weather is extremely unpredictable, and we have no shelter from the sun and—oh yes—no ocean."

So we set out to create an Ohio version of that baptism on the beach. Our discipleship team held baptism classes as our makeover team began designing an event that would rival that Hawaiian cele-

bration. Two huge big-top tents were rented to house a cookout for the guest families. Lay pastors and servants were recruited to perform the baptisms, and special arrangements were made for registration, certificates, and even a tent for photos with the pastor (families loved this).

We borrowed bushes and trees from a local landscaping business and dug through our outdoor décor stash to complement the occasion's design. I'm happy to report that our makeover team did a fabulous job creating an environment that almost made you forget that our water source was, in fact, a big blue blow-up pool.

Change the World Pop-Up Bookstores

Ginghamsburg's call to be a teaching church has taken many forms over the years, and we generally host at least one conference a year to help resource and support that initiative. One of my very favorite projects is creating a "pop-up" bookstore to support our Change the World Conference. I love pulling a cohesive design out of the theme of the conference and gathering the team and furnishings to execute those concepts. The bookstore "pops up" in the back area of our worship center, just inside the coffee shop. It's like

creating a world inside a world, and it emerges as great community space where conference guests can hang out, mingle, and browse. Sure, we don't really have designated bookstore "space," but with a bit of mud 'n spit, we suddenly see the potential of what we can creatively transform.

If necessity is truly the mother of invention, creativity must be the dad. I hope you've enjoyed this tour showcasing community spaces—results of what necessity plus creative energy can together produce.

In the back corner of your mind you may have a few questions about the process, including, perhaps, "I see what your team has accomplished, but how did you get

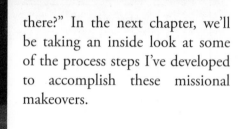

there?" In the next chapter, we'll be taking an inside look at some of the process steps I've developed to accomplish these missional makeovers.

Chapter 6

EXECUTE YOUR CONCEPT

The mission of Jesus is often messy, costly, and inconvenient.

—Mike Slaughter

Makeover momentum is gained not by taking on the remodeling of your entire church building at once, but rather by creating a strategy to move steadily forward, room by room. And it's going to take some time to grow your wings and gain some confidence. This is where it might be a good idea to share some of my best learning experiences so that you can be a little further ahead than I was at the beginning.

Overseeing makeovers is a lot like being a building contractor in the real world. The difference in my case is that most of the workers are servants, not hired employees. *Unpaid* servants give up hours of time many weeks in hopes of making a real difference—and they do.

The creative process is messy, difficult, and usually takes twice as long as we think it will. Just when we get the hang of each new treatment, it's time to move on to another seemingly impossible task. The entire process requires a lot of patience, positivity, and the cemented commitment to finish well.

Listen—Invent—Personalize

As the founder and CEO of Amazon.com, Inc., Jeff Bezos led the company to become the largest retailer on the Internet. Many years ago I read an article that outlined Jeff's strategy for successful customer connection in three words: *listen, invent,* and *personalize*. Since that time I've used that same strategy as I interact with ministry partners, staff, and pastors who have new space needs.

Listening to your "customer" is a vital step that can save much time and money later on. For instance, in the case of a classroom redesign, I would ask the ministry leader to name all the possible ways the room will be used. Does the room function more as a classroom? Will there be the desire to use the room in a conversational setting that requires casual seating, low coffee tables, and soft, ambient lighting? How many people will we need to fit into this room at any given time?

If it's an office being redesigned, I ask what kind of work environment the staff person requires. Quiet? Open? Would he or she function better with the desk facing the door or facing the wall? Will he or she need a team-meeting space or simply seating for one guest?

If the space redesign requires updating a large part of a church building, I ask the pastor to describe the DNA of the church body: the mission, demographic, and tangible community needs and desires. How is the current space not working to support its current mission and role? What is the budget for the redesign? What space cannot yet change?

Invention is my favorite part of the strategy, but I strive to invent mindfully, reusing all possible existing furnishings, keeping an eye on budget restrictions, and assuring that this new design will stand the test of time.

Invention pulls together color schemes, material samples, and a proposed floor plan in response to the needs represented. I then usually create a physical "design board" that will be a shared "template" to inform all decisions going forward.

Personalizing the design takes the form of *maximizing* the details as we move toward completion. How can we make this space uniquely styled for the occasion or person? What story will the details tell? How can we take the new furnishings and arrange them in such a way as to draw guests in? How can we finish the design in such a way that the DNA and the story are told throughout the space? Wall hangings, unique décor items, and furniture will be the final touches that personalize and maximize the design.

Whether for longtime saints or well-intentioned sinners, the reality of change can be difficult to manage. Still, there are some steps I've learned to help other leaders and ministry partners come along, support, and help champion the process. Here are a few pointers I've gleaned from my alma mater, the School of Hard Knocks.

Be a Solution Finder

Any job worth doing is going to bring with it a host of challenges, and some will seem insurmountable. Actually, I can't think of a single makeover project during which I wasn't tempted to have at least one meltdown. Staying in meltdown mode is bad form for leadership and certainly doesn't advance the project forward. I've learned to take a moment to privately pull myself together and shift as quickly as possible into solution mode. If I can't think of a solution for a significant challenge on my own, I choose one or two servants from the team to huddle with me and brainstorm solutions. Engaging our collective thoughts, coupled with those prayers of despera-

tion, almost always yields workable, if not astonishing, results. The key is to hang in there until the solution—aka the "miracle"—appears. It will.

Be Approachable: "Can Do!"

No one wants to work with Debbie Downer, least of all me. I don't want to be Debbie Downer either, come to think of it. Keeping a positive, approachable spirit is vitally important to the morale of any team and in the end builds trust in my design abilities. Maintaining a positive, upbeat working atmosphere will also keep people coming back to serve over and over again. Even when I'm not at all sure how we'll accomplish a difficult task, who will be available to do it, or when we'll find the time, I keep moving forward in faith, trusting God will provide and confidently trust in "can do!"

Serve with Generosity

As a campus designer, I've been entrusted with the funds, furniture, and freedom to manage a great deal of environmental supplies. Rather than exhibiting a spirit of protection, I've learned to make it a point to accommodate all ministry needs and requests possible. I reuse, repurpose, and refurbish as time permits so that when there's a need for candles, fabric, building materials, or décor supplies, chances are I have it and you are welcome to use it. We incorporate a library system of borrowing and returning supplies, with the goal that all our events, dinners, classes, and spaces share the wealth of engaging environments.

Don't Let Lack of Funds Limit the Dreams

Our staff had gathered in the worship area for a monthly chapel over lunch. The pastor who was leading that day asked us to discuss this question with our table groups: If money was no object, what would you want to do to move the mission forward at Ginghamsburg?

The responses that ensued were nothing short of fascinating. I had no idea my coworkers were dreaming those kind of dreams! Ginghamsburg generally runs on a very tight budget so that we are able to give generously toward outreach and mission. Listening to the staff responses that day, I realized that we may be shortchanging some of our dreams, assuming we can't afford them anyway—so what's the use in dreaming?

That day is a reminder for me to keep praying prayers of possibility. Keep pushing forward, and keep dreaming about what God wants to do in our community. If God is in it, the provision will follow. If we quit dreaming, we might preempt the God movement. Carl Sandburg wisely stated, "Nothing happens but first a dream."

Summing up this approach to creative expression, I prefer to believe I've been freed up, not to be Ginghamsburg's design gestapo, announcing what staff can and can't do in their offices, events, and ministry spaces, but rather to be empowered as a servant, gifted and anointed to encourage my coworkers to discover solutions and innovations that will lead to their best ministry success.

Managing Projects

Here is a list of the steps I strive to take as I manage each makeover project. Whether for a classroom makeover, a stage design, a staged event, or an office update, the process is much the same.

Collect Input

Listen, take notes, and do the research. Use research, home improvement stores, and experts in the field. Learn all you can up front.

Navigate Ideas with Grace

People will give you their opinions, and that is fine. You don't have to respond to every idea. Take it all in, consider your options, and gracefully move forward without criticizing the extra ideas.

Recruit, Schedule, Confirm, and Connect

This was covered in chapter 4, "Ignite Your Community," but even after the project begins, you will need to stay in touch with servants coming and going and changes in schedules and plans. Anything less can become frustrating to the teammates you value so much.

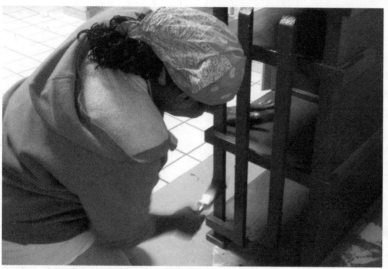

Inventory and Purchase the Supplies

Although there may be times when you can task a trusted teammate to purchase materials, you will need to be the one to assure the right supplies are ready when the workers arrive. This can all be done ahead of time so that the work hours can be spent on the job and not running back and forth to the store.

Prepare the Space/Secure the Tools

Once again, you will be smart to delegate some of the pieces of each project to capable teammates, but do be sure that the space has been secured during the duration of the project and that the tools are ready to roll. Ladders? Scaffolding? Drills? Sawhorses? While some of these tools are available on our campus, most of them come in by way of the servants, who often prefer

using their own familiar tools and equipment anyway.

Remember the Food

Whenever a project spans a mealtime, I think ahead about how we will handle the hunger. My rule of thumb is to ask servants to pack their own lunches for the first meal. If we are working over two mealtimes, I furnish that second meal—usually dinner—by ordering pizza or preparing a home-cooked meal. It's been wonderful on occasion to have a servant who can't work the project to offer to provide the meal. Several times my life group has contributed a full meal for a huge project. It means a lot to the makeover team if we can sit down to talk and eat together if possible—even for just a few minutes.

Sketch the Plans

I'm often tempted to keep the plans in my head; after all, *I* know what they are! Results will multiply, however, when you can physically sketch a plan or picture on paper and explain it to key team players, allowing them to see and contribute more powerfully to the final picture.

Be Decisive

You are the leader and won't be doing anyone a favor by failing to make critical decisions. Having a wishy-washy or falsely humble attitude can wind up wasting valuable time for you and your team. Confident leader equals confident team.

Oversee the Project without Micromanaging the Tasks

Larger makeover projects need someone to keep watch over the entire process, assuring that all servants have what they need to succeed. If you dive into any one aspect too deep, you won't be available for all. Assign tasks, and then stay available for any input and answers needed.

Encourage and Coach

Say it often, and say it loud: "Great job, guys!" "Looking awesome, ladies!" Everyone likes to hear they are doing a good job, and saying so out loud keeps a positive, uplifting atmosphere for everyone in the room.

Allow Time for Cleaning Up

Depending on the scope of the project, the time to clean up must never be underestimated. Keeping in mind the promised ending time, begin the cleanup well in advance. Failure to plan ahead will leave that final action to—guess who?—you. And if you let that happen, you will leave bone tired with a martyr's complex (not good)!

Secure Space for Storage

Securing a well-organized storage space that stays clean and functional is something we work at every single week. When the goods to be stored outweigh the space available, I call in an expert to suggest some new storage systems. It's also fine to ask gifted servants to come serve by cleaning and reorganizing. Out of sight is out of mind, and out of mind means it won't get used again, which is poor stewardship.

Be the Last Cowboy (or Girl) on the Trail

Most times you will need to make the final inspection to assure that the workspace is cleaned, tools are put away, lights and music are off, and doors are locked. You'll sleep better knowing things were left just as you would like to find them.

EXECUTE YOUR CONCEPT | 47

Share the Love

Once that project is complete and the compliments start rolling in, be sure to pass them on to your team. Always be sure to share the credit for team projects, knowing that your reward is not here on earth anyway. Take every opportunity to let your teammates know how valuable their contribution has become.

PART III

STEEPLES TO STARBUCKS: REIMAGINING WORSHIP SPACES

The LORD God's spirit is upon me,
because the LORD has anointed me.
He has sent me
to bring good news to the poor,
to bind up the brokenhearted,
to proclaim release for captives, and liberation for prisoners.

—Isaiah 61:1

Have you ever attended a worship or leadership conference somewhat inspired, yet quietly confused? We see how others are "doing it." We've observed their talent and the great ways God is using them. We've written down everything the speakers had to say. We've made real decisions to do things better. Yet even in the wake of this wave of inspiration, we experience a disconnection. "How am I supposed to replicate what they're doing? How is our church going to take all the necessary steps to become like their church?"

As I journey with Jesus, this comparison complex has given me pause, and I now believe that to attempt to replicate another worship leader's or church's DNA would be a slap in the face to the One who has "fearfully and wonderfully" made each of us. Our creator God has given each one of us a unique package. *The Message* translates it this way: "Whoever did want him, who believed he was who he claimed and would do what he said, he made to be their true selves, their child-of-God selves" (John 1:12 THE MESSAGE). I celebrate the theology of different strokes for different church folks. Thankfully, there is no one size, shape, color, or design blueprint for what a great church can look like, as long as it centers on the ultimate truth that Jesus is Lord.

At some point, however, each faith community must identify the piece of the mission God has called them to and then set out to execute that vision in tangible ways. As the campus designer at Ginghamsburg Church, I've spent a few years etching out a ministry role that is being invented as we go along. One of the great privileges I've had in recent years is to serve as space-design consultant for a diverse array of churches that most often have been in some sort of season of transition—a new vision or God movement consequentially requiring spatial support. Many times my role is to temporarily partner with the leadership team of that faith community to create customized space where new lives will find a relationship with God through Jesus.

These faith communities exhibit a wide variety of complexions, a vast difference in "callings," every style ranging from a brand-new church plant to the traditional, stained-glass structures seeking to reach out in new ways to an old neighborhood. In this part, I'm looking forward to sharing three basic design categories identified from eight different and unique ministries. I've invited leaders from each of these locations to share the vision behind their redesign, what God is doing, and how the newly designed spaces are supporting that vision.

Chapter 7

New Church Plants: Simply Welcoming Environments

Start by doing what's necessary; then do what's possible; and suddenly you are doing the impossible.

—*St. Francis of Assisi*

I've observed good and bad news about church planting. The good news is the fresh slate of ministry, unencumbered by all the baggage that years of unhealthy history in established churches can bring, allowing the core leaders to dream freely. The bad news is that—at the onset—there is seldom enough funding for all those amazing dreams to take root. That being said, the momentum of Jesus followers out on the front edge of making brand-new disciples creates an exciting, designable atmosphere.

While visiting our daughter and son-in-law, who were living for a year in Helena, Montana, my family and I attended a fairly new church plant together, Narrate Church (narratechurch.org). This new faith community was meeting in a small, older downtown Helena theater that had a quaintness about it despite the tight quarters. What struck me was how well the space had been customized for that weekend worship experience. Professional signage was placed at strategic locations, an impromptu coffee bar awaited customers on the way to the children's area, and a very intentional, welcoming vibe being communicated was unmistakably *now*. What a great worship hour we enjoyed that day. That little faith community had all the right elements to send them soaring, poised to attract new seekers and to grow.

Helping provide physical space insight for new church plants at the onset of their journeys has been a great adventure for me. I've noted that despite the locations being quite different, the basic elements required for design success are very much the same. Great signage, clean and tasteful spaces for adults and children, and a state-of-the-art coffee feature all combine to create simply welcoming environments. Listen in to what a few of those pioneering pastors have to say.

The Gathering, Middletown, Ohio

Pastor Carrie Jena

The Vision

The United Methodist Gathering began as a third worship service in the basement of First United Methodist in Middletown, Ohio, in February of 2007. In March of 2011, we moved out of the basement and into a storefront location in the center of the downtown mission field. The initial goal of the Gathering was to reach the unchurched, urban population of Middletown that includes the poor, unemployed, homeless, mentally ill, and addicted living in the downtown area. Since our launch, however, we have attracted people from all economic backgrounds who want to be part of a church that is missional in its theology and practice. Our two Sunday morning worship services, six weekly small groups, Bible studies, discipleship strategies, and community outreach events are all designed to reflect a missional emphasis—sending us into the community to make disciples and to effectively serve the poor in ways that change lives. Our core values reflect our desire to grow disciples and to offer a church community that is authentic, accountable, relevant, and missional.

The Redesign

When we moved from the basement of the church to our own site on Central Avenue, we called Kim and asked her to help us design a space that would be welcoming to the urban community that we serve and that would reflect our core values. Kim's first decision was to hang large poster-sized black-and-white photos of some of the people in our congregation to help guests feel welcome and to give them faces that they might recognize. Kim's second recommendation was to put large-lettered words on the walls that reflected

our core values: missional, authentic, relevant, and accountable. Instead of using pews, we incorporated small round tables with candles in the center that helped foster relationships among the people—particularly among those who came from the homeless shelters and had no family or significant relationships in their life. Since incorporating Kim's design strategies, our church grew from 75 people to an average of 110 in worship. In Easter of 2012, we chartered as an independent United Methodist church and moved into a new larger space,

still in downtown Middletown. In the next few months we will remove a wall that will enable us to double our worship space and erect two new walls to create a better flow on Sunday mornings. We will be using many of Kim's design recommendations in our new space, including adding several furniture "pods," maintaining a relaxed atmosphere for small groups and Bible studies, using warm colors in the sanctuary, setting up a coffee/conversation area adjacent to the worship space, and implementing lighting and other design techniques in our worship space.

Kim's note: The UM Gathering space also includes a wonderful children's room, ample restroom space, and a modest kitchen prep area; it is a simply welcoming environment ready to embrace the least and the lost.

The Village Church, Toledo, Ohio

Pastor Cheri Holdridge

The Vision

Long before the Pew Research Center published their 2012 study, "Nones on the Rise: One in Five Adults Have No Religious Affiliation," the Village Church Toledo came into being in order to reach the "nones" of northwest Ohio and southeast Michigan. Many of these folks call themselves spiritual but not religious because they have become disillusioned with organized religion. So, we put up a sign out front that says: "The Village Church, come try us, we're not very organized!" Many of the people we are reaching self-identify as progressives; they are mostly left of center politically. They don't understand why some churches exclude gay, lesbian, bisexual, and transgender people, because Jesus loved everyone. Our church has a clear value: we dare to welcome all people. Some might call us the misfits or people living on the edge of society. We just call ourselves the Village People (pun intended).

We love to serve. One of the values we hold dear is to get out into the community and to serve at the local food bank or this past year inviting women and children affected by domestic violence to join us for lunch on Mother's Day. Parents like to bring their kids to our church because they can serve alongside their children in our community. Our vision is to follow Jesus and change the world. We are doing our best in our little part of the world in Toledo, Ohio. We believe we are making a difference.

The Redesign

Space is crucial to my ministry. To date I have asked Kim Miller to consult on redesigns for my church at three different junctures when we've outgrown our old space. Each time she helps in big and small ways to bring a sense of simplicity and welcome to the space. Once when bringing her makeover team for a work weekend, she decorated a bathroom in a bar that we converted into a church. I said afterward, "No one is going to leave this church for the first time and say, 'That was the nicest bathroom I have ever been in. I am going back to that church.' But they will come back undoubtedly because the entire space was so warm and inviting." Kim helps teams create these sorts of spaces.

Our current worship space is a small movie theater with movable round tables and chairs. Kim and her husband, Clark, came for a consult to help us find simple ways to make the theater feel like our Village every Sunday morning. She worked with the colors and plants already in the theater and the rug we'd added to the mix. Then she advised my team about creating inexpensive table decorations that could be changed out by the seasons. She helped us find a designer who could create some professional freestanding banners to stand in the front of our "worship area" to frame the band. We use a high-top table for any additional items such as Communion elements or candles. The large movie screen, with PowerPoint, provides the backdrop. In our hospitality area, we have continuity with the colors and themes of the table decorations in the worship space. We created a small welcome center, again with excellent signage. Our biggest expense—and the best money spent—was on attractive outdoor directional signs that welcome people to our worship space from any entrance to the theater. This is so important when you are meeting in a space that you are using only one day of the week. We also got creative with fabric by fastening it to the walls with

Velcro each week in order to create an inviting space for our children. A nice rug and some pillows transform an extra-wide hallway into a fun and inviting space for kids.

For the Village, signage and hospitality toward people of all ages are essential in making the space inviting. People show up thinking they are going to be in a sterile movie theater, and they are surprised that the place feels more like a cozy coffeehouse. On Sundays when our band starts playing, God shows up, and we have church!

Chapter 8

TRADITIONAL CHURCH TRANSFORMATIONS

Creativity involves breaking out of established patterns in order to look at things in a different way.

—Edward de Bono

True confession: There was a time when I thought that traditional church buildings had had their day. Stained-glass windows, bare wood floors, and tall, cavernous ceilings all spoke to me of an earlier era, no longer relevant enough for present-day ministry. I'm happy to say that I've completely outgrown that way of thinking, discovering that by incorporating a few tasteful and trendy upgrades, this same space can feature the absolute best of both worlds.

There are a few challenges intrinsic to older, more traditional church buildings, however. Often worship and classroom space abound, but true community-friendly "lobby" or "sit down and relax and just be yourself" space is scarce. The main entrances can be uninviting for new guests, and the "flow" between various areas can be convoluted, not to mention handicapped-inaccessible. Guest signage is usually minimal to nonexistent. The longer a congregation inhabits the same building, the more difficult it is to see the environment through the eyes of new guests.

Despite these challenges, I have done a "design 180" and wholeheartedly believe there are working solutions ready to be discovered in each situation. Keep reading to learn the stories told by church leaders of traditional church buildings transformed for modern-day ministry.

Fort McKinley Church, Dayton, Ohio

Pastor Dave Hood

The Vision

Five years ago, Fort McKinley was a dying inner-city church that had long since lost connection with the community that surrounded it. When the neighborhood changed, the church was unable to change with it and began to die. The forty white people who were left had a heart for the community but no effective strategy for outreach and no leader who could show the way. They knew changes were necessary but did not know which changes to make or how to make them.

In 2008, Fort McKinley merged with Ginghamsburg Church, and I was appointed to make the changes necessary for this handful of people to reach the community and become a vital center of empowerment and transformation once again. Everything changed; the music became more indigenous to the diverse community, the dress code relaxed, and the building underwent a complete makeover with updates and touches much more welcoming and familiar to the community as the focus turned from an inward-survival mode to an outward-seeking mode.

Today, Fort McKinley is a growing and thriving center of faith and life in the Dayton community. Weekend worship averages more than 450 in attendance, with another 100 children and 40 youth packing the education wing. According to our conference bishop, more African Americans attend Fort McKinley church than any other United Methodist church in all of Ohio, and that is only 50 percent of our congregation.

But what is happening inside the building is only half the story; it is what is happening in the community that is the real miracle. Through partnership and network building, Fort McKinley Church has been the catalyst responsible for building twenty-five new homes for lower-income families inside the fifteen neighborhood blocks. Two additional Habitat for Humanity homes have been built, with more in the works. A community garden has been created, maintained, and supported and a pavilion built where families can gather. The local former firehouse has been renovated into a community center and youth ministry space. The church has also taken on such big issues as education and employment, with a focus on partnerships with local schools and GED programs. This year we added Jobs for Life, a class that trains potential employees and partners them with great employers. Fort McKinley Church is truly living into its vision to become the empowering and transforming center of the community.

The Redesign

Before the physical transformation of the Fort McKinley church building, it was perfectly suited to welcome 1950s suburban, middle-class people—and it was suburban, middle-class people who were still coming. The problem was that the environment was unfamiliar, unwelcoming, and disconnected from the expectations of those who currently live in our community. Quilts, banners, and memorial plaques were all artifacts that meant something to the current attendees but conveyed a different message to those who were not yet connected. Through some intentional "urbanizing" and updating, we were able to communicate to our neighbors that we were making an intentional effort to welcome them and speak their language.

There were also some theological redesigns that needed to be made. The giant oak pulpit and lectern that stood as behemoths separating the church leadership from the congregation were torn out, and a stage that brought the preacher out into the room and toward the people was designed and installed. This renovation drastically changed our ability to communicate effectively with our new guests who were beginning to attend.

In this community that struggles so much with the results of

poverty and neglect, places that are clean and sharp are unique and rare. A new coat of paint on the walls, updated furniture in the children's spaces, some sharpening of signage, and

tasteful décor have all made a huge difference to those who live in our neighborhood. The fresh environment gives new life pictures and conveys a sense that "these people have something I want" or "these people know something I need to know." It's a contagious atmosphere in which people want to connect.

Lakewood United Methodist Church, Lakewood, Ohio

Pastor Laura Jaissle (serving with Pastor Bruce Hartley)

The Vision

Our community in Lakewood, Ohio, is very diverse, with lots of young adults and young families, 80 percent of whom are unchurched. Lakewood UMC is a huge, beautiful old structure with a congregation that has developed a long history of missional involvement with a strong presence in the community for more than 135 years. During the past few years, we have recommitted ourselves to increasing this active presence.

For many years Lakewood had only one worship service. Since the 1970s, like that of many mainline denominations, worship attendance at LUMC had been declining. In 2009, LUMC launched an alternative, more contemporary worship service, with a live band called Impact, in Daniels Hall, the basement of the church. This brought new life and energy to Lakewood Church, but Impact was outgrowing its basement location, and Lakewood's new growth was suffocating. With the addition of this new service, the church had recommitted to going beyond the walls of the building to serve those in the community.

It also became obvious to the church community that we have an amazing building that is a huge asset to our community and that we need to be able to share it with more people through worship and community outreach and events.

The Redesign

Realizing the felt needs of the congregation and the surrounding community, Lakewood began to explore ways the sanctuary space could be reconfigured to better meet the needs of an ever-changing community and a new generation of believers. It was through this process that we contacted Kim and Clark Miller to come to Lakewood and observe and give our church a recommendation regarding how we could best use our worship space. Kim gave our church a comprehensive set of recommendations that became a starting point for our Lakewood team to create a viable concept, equipping our congregation with the ability to consider and adopt the recommendations and then to move forward.

The blessing of the worship space concept that was eventually accepted by the congregation was that it would enable the spacious sanctuary to house the traditional worship service as well as the alternative Impact service. It would allow our most beautiful space to be used for more than one hour on Sunday morning. In addition, by removing some of the physical barriers on the large stage, the choir and speakers will function closer to the audience, increasing the sense of community we desire. We anticipate that the Impact service will benefit, growing into what is a more sacred and welcoming worship space.

The goal is for this redesign to empower our church to reach more effectively into our community, offering three distinct but fully supported styles of worship: an early Sunday contemplative chapel service (including Communion), a traditional midmorning worship featuring a full chancel choir, and the Impact worship service that meets late morning with a livelier band-led atmosphere. There is a history of change and evolution at Lakewood UMC, a history of transforming itself to reach the current needs of the community; and this is the exciting next phase in the life of LUMC.

Newark Nazarene Church (The Naz), Newark, Ohio

Worship and Music Pastor Brian Redman

The Vision

God has done an amazing thing at Newark Naz over the last twelve years, taking something that was stuck, broken, and dead and doing what God does best—breathe life, strength, and beauty back into it. It's really a story that we hear and see so many times: God restores what was lost. And our church was lost. Our vision and call were barely beating. But through new, strong leadership, a clear vision, and a people willing to lay down their own preferences, God began to work. Our mission statement is simple: leading people into a growing relationship with Christ. But how we carry out that mission

has been the joy of my ministry. It is incredible to see God at work as we celebrate God's presence in worship, strengthening our lives in community and living out our call to love and serve our church and neighbors.

Part of our calling has been to "stay in the hood." We've had a few opportunities to move outside the city of Newark and build a nice multimillion-dollar building, but instead, we felt God calling us to be the hands and feet of Christ to our present neighborhood. In the past, we really didn't have much of an influence in our community but felt God strongly calling us to change our hearts and vision. Because of that decision, we have had to figure out how to meet the needs of a growing church with over one thousand in attendance each weekend. To help meet that challenge, we arranged for multiple services (one on Saturday night and three on Sunday morning), while opening up two other nearby sites (video venues) and redesigning our worship spaces.

The Redesign

Our church building's last revision was in 1968, so we were overdue for a redesign. We recently renovated two spaces: our worship space/sanctuary and the lobby. Even though the space seats around four hundred people, we wanted to create a warmer, informal, and inviting feel that sends the message "We are doing this thing together." The stage is not too "stagey." Warm colors, soft lighting, and scents of flickering candles dominate the senses. Natural wood walls and beams left exposed on the sides of the stage enhance this feeling as well. At Kim's suggestion, we changed the

harsh, cold gray brick wall that stared down at the congregation by painting it white, hanging an amazing wood cross in the middle, and throwing up some vibrant color using lighting cans. This has become the focal point during worship.

We removed barriers between the congregation and stage—altars, rails, lecterns, choir pews—and extended the stage out toward the people to help create a feeling of "together" instead a feeling of "us and them." We removed the media/sound booth from the back of the room and built a loft, affording us more space for seating. We also chose smaller side screens to help with the more intimate feel.

After all is said and done, the space that we've designed has helped our church family, allowing us to enter a place that speaks peace to our senses and souls and also helps focus our thoughts on a personal God in an atmosphere that is "real" and "familiar." My personal motto—which I believe I stole from Kim—is that I want our worship space to look and feel like Pier 1, not Walmart.

We also did a major redesign in our lobby. The previous lobby was so cozy that no one wanted to leave and go into the sanctuary! Our challenge was to open up the space and keep it looking and feeling intimate but not too homey. So, we knocked out some walls; built a new entry; put in a café, new flooring, and bigger stairways; and gave everything an incredible "lodge" feel. We really opened up the space but kept some aspects looking and feeling intimate.

One of the most frequent compliments we receive from our visitors sounds something like, "This church felt warm and loving from the minute I walked inside. When the music and worship started, I just couldn't quit weeping. God was so present to me." It's amazing what our simple redesigns have done to help foster this feeling of worshipful intimacy.

An old thing becomes new if you detach it from what usually surrounds it. (Robert Bresson)

Chapter 9

COFFEE-SHOP ENVIRONMENTS: REIMAGINING THE TABLE OF GOD

While they were eating, Jesus took bread, blessed it, broke it, and gave it to the disciples and said, "Take and eat. This is my body." He took a cup, gave thanks, and gave it to them, saying, "Drink from this, all of you."

—Matthew 26:26-27

Let it be said that I *love* coffee shops. Several years ago my closest salvage sister, Robin, my husband, Clark, and I made a four-hour round-trip excursion once a week for two months to remodel my brother's college-town coffee shop in Granville, Ohio. Painting, sanding, laying new floor, adding new furnishings, and reupholstering old chairs in this century-old mansion was crazy, hardworking fun. Even though the work was rewarding and the truck talks to and fro were wonderful, the real motivation that kept us going back was simple. We loved being in that warm coffee-shop atmosphere. The colors, the smells, and that sweet café ambience all drew us back, week after week.

While working on this book I took my laptop into a Tipp City coffee shop where I could write alone with only occasional passing interactions with other customers. During my two-hour visit, I overheard many heart-to-heart conversations—people sharing in a relaxed manner—not with a therapist or a preacher, but with a trusted coffee-date friend. Is it any wonder that more and more churches—seeking to create spaces for connection and community—are finding ways to build a coffee-bar function into their lobbies and community spaces? We've finally "gotten" what AA groups have known for decades: that men and women talk, share, and let down their guard just a little bit better when holding a cup of warmth in their hands. Perhaps it's true that real-life change happens not in rows but in circles—and often around a table.

Ideally, the best plan would be to start fresh and incorporate coffee-shop space into any new church-building project. That way there would be plenty of coffee space and a state-of-the-art supporting-kitchen component. Unfortunately, few of us are working with ideal conditions, yet that doesn't have to be a showstopper. Every single church I've consulted in the last several years has received and implemented the recommendation of a coffee-area feature in some way, shape, or form. A

large counter in the lobby and pews removed from the back of the traditional worship area create that extra space for conversation. A church-basement alternative worship space can have chairs arranged around café tables. A coat closet off the lobby can be transformed into a cozy coffee-shop corner.

Ironically, one of the most limiting configurations for coffee-shop space was at our own Ginghamsburg campus. We'd furnished a nice student coffee shop in our activities building, but truthfully most adults never made the awkward coffee trek across the parking lot to that building during the weekend worship times, regrettably losing the opportunity for community connections. It's not that we didn't want a coffee shop in our main building; the needed space hadn't been accommodated into the original building design and simply wasn't to be found—or so we thought.

Then we found the space. It had been there all along: a worship overflow room we'd turned into a bookstore, where sales had waned because of electronic book sales. The plumbing necessary for a coffee shop wasn't too far down the hall, and the extra traffic-flow space we needed was obtained by knocking out the two corner walls adjacent to the hallway. Now we're talking! We designed this new space with a small bookstore feature, and this coffee hub is now abuzz with customers all week long! Preschool parents, building guests, staff, and servants are

finding connection during the week, while worship attendees are discovering community space on the weekends. Even if you don't like coffee, you can't complain about the distinctive roasted aroma and added excitement in the air.

We did not have seating space inside the new coffee shop, so I suggested we think of our entire worship and lobby spaces as space for seating. We replaced the boxy counters in our main lobby with tall bistro tables and stools and removed rows of chairs along the back of our worship area for this trendy seating option. Most people prefer relaxed seating choices to the traditional church pews, and theoretically there's always room for a tasteful combination of both.

Pastor Dave Hood, from our Fort McKinley campus, tells about his newest café church environment, the Point:

As our Fort McKinley congregation began to grow past what three Sunday worship times could hold, we looked at acquiring another campus fifteen miles down the road. We believe that lack of space doesn't

excuse us from Jesus' Great Commission to "go into the whole world and proclaim the good news to every creature" (Mark 16:15), so we began looking for a location to plant a new faith community.

On Easter 2012, less than four years after we restarted Fort McKinley, we planted the Point in a small shopping plaza in the neighboring community of Trotwood. Initially, Kim surmised that the Fort and the Point were polar opposites of each other in terms of design. The Fort building was structurally sound yet chopped up in terms of traffic flow and ease of accessibility. Conversely, the Point had a great flow—all on one level, air-conditioned, and easy to access—but was cheaply built, with various structural issues such as a leaky roof and poorly constructed walls—poorly constructed pink walls, that is.

That purple-pink color was everywhere: the worship area, the large hallways, and even the ceilings!

Kim recruited servant teams to renovate the space with a design plan that made sense in that city environment. We redesigned the worship area with colors more conducive to the urban feel of the community, applying a skyline design to the back stage wall as an ongoing reminder of our commitment to the city. Our children's director, Erica Sharp, coordinated a team to cover the children's areas with paint, murals, and updated furnishings until it buzzed with freshness and fun. We had identified our largest target audience to be

families with children, so we knew these spaces had to be excellent. Best of all, we transformed the large main entry space into a guest-friendly café area with plenty of four-top tables and chairs and a coffee counter. Kim's design included new colors to match the new mood.

Pastor Dave reports that after just six months, the Point averaged more than 120 in worship every Saturday night, with an additional 40 children. The worship area gives a club feel that people describe as "very welcoming."

Every Saturday night after the planned worship gathering, the café area hosts a second vibrant gathering where families pack together around tables, eating and connecting with one another in an environment that is conducive to relationship building. The café area is so popular that we are now attempting to re-create that same type of space at our campuses as well.

As I wrap up this diverse tour of transformations, I hope you are thinking of your own church-community spaces. Which category most closely mimics your own? And what are the possibilities for transformation in your own setting? What an exciting opportunity we have ahead to push out all the possibilities for redesigning the spaces we've been given.

PART IV

STAGE DESIGN

Now when Jesus saw the crowds, he went up a mountain. He sat down and his disciples came to him.

—Matthew 5:1

Great communication always requires a stage. According to the Gospel accounts, Jesus found himself on a stage quite often. Sometimes that stage took the form of a boat or a hillside—or a boat looking up at a hillside. Other times we see Jesus taking a seat in a lunchroom or at a dining room table, or standing on the coffee table in an absolutely jam-packed living room. Whether poised atop a large rock or up in front of a temple courtyard, Jesus could command the attention of an audience of rowdy hecklers, directing all eyes toward the compelling message at hand.

Whether your church is a large cathedral-like structure or a coffee shop downtown, you will also find yourself asking how and where to feature the messengers (preacher, speaker, music makers) and how to present your theme in such a way as to create the very best environment for communication. No book on creating community spaces would be complete without a significant portion on stage design. As I describe some of our most recent stage designs at Ginghamsburg in the following pages, don't be afraid to imagine how you might give your message just the right setting to further transform the lives of the members of your worshiping community.

Chapter 10

ROOM WITH A VIEW

A vision is not just a picture of what could be;
it is an appeal to our better selves,
a call to become something more.

—*Rosabeth Moss Kanter*

It occurs to me that all faith communities have a certain set of common needs when considering worship spaces. Worship venues usually have a raised-floor stage component built in somewhere. Almost every worship setting includes worship leaders, speaker-preachers, and sometimes readings or sketches requiring physical space. All of these components need to be seen to be effective. At the same time, worship nearly always includes a music component—a simple piano, an organ, oftentimes an entire band, vocalists, and occasionally even a choir. Space is needed for all. More and more, media pieces are being integrated into worship experiences, so eventually a screen is imposed into this montage of stage components. The challenge is how to arrange all of these diverse special entities in a tasteful manner.

In addition, how a stage "fits" the room, how accessible it feels, and how visually appealing it is all make a huge difference in the overall effectiveness or "mood" of the worship space. There are a total of seven stages on Ginghamsburg's four campuses, and each one represents a different challenge and subsequent solution to right-sizing the feel of the room.

The main building worship space on our Tipp City campus seats about six hundred people, not including the overflow rooms on both the main floor and the upper level, which can seat about three hundred more. Not wanting to be limited by this midsized room, we've offered five worship times each weekend nearly the entire time we've been in the building.

Just this past summer, after many years of inhabiting this building, we felt the large velvet theatrical-looking curtains that ran across the stage were feeling old, dark, and dingy. In addition, they weren't really part of the band-driven worship vibe we now embrace. This past summer we contracted to have them removed, and our makeover team set out to accommodate this fresh, clean start by building new stage steps and side panels and creating an accessible, wide-open stage design. The difference is so remarkable we can't figure out why we waited

this long to remove the curtains. The stage feels wider and subsequently more connected to the expanse of the congregation seated in the room; it is a cleaner, more up-to-date look. We'll talk more about this stage design in the section "Four-Letter Words."

The Avenue—our student-ministry activity center—holds a large gym stage so deep and high that it felt inaccessible for many years. Once commissioned, our makeover team partnered with our student staff team to design our way into a much more useful and aesthetically pleasing approach. We built four large stage flats: two to flank each side of the stage (large screen in the center back), allowing for the flats to be staged in a number of configurations. One design can be applied to one side of the flats, and a second to the opposite side, allowing for great artistic flexibility.

The stage in our Fort McKinley building was the most traditional church style, and the rebuilding of that worship space was described in chapter 8. The Point stage—described in chapter 9—features a great advantage in its wide expanse, but the ceiling was quite low, which gave the room a very oppressive, unprofessional feeling. In order to right-size that challenge, we painted the entire ceiling black and tore out the tiles above the stage. Once all the hardware, cables, and exposed fixtures were painted black, it emerged as quite a legitimate worship space, one that we felt

would more closely suit the demographic preferences of those in the neighborhood.

In general, stages should be as wide or nearly as wide as the room and just high enough for visual accessibility, with graduated steps—or at least easy access. Any means of bridging the chasm between "us" and "them" is a good thing. Café seating in front, Communion tables set closer, a lower stage extension, and steps that appear to be as one with the stage all invite worshipers into the experience generated from the stage.

Simply Beautiful: The Stained-Glass Stage

Before we dive into talking about full-blown stage design, I want to state a disclaimer. I don't believe all worship spaces are conducive to the all-out, thematic stage-design makeovers that we do at our Tipp City campus. Some sanctuaries are already rich with visual texture: stained-glass windows, well-crafted woodwork, and architecture that whispers a story all its own. In these cases, I would add seasonal candles or perhaps a well-displayed large prop on the stage, ready to add visual interest and clarity when highlighted. Weekly changes do create a sense of anticipation, however. Simple, fresh flowers, candles flickering softly, the sight and sound of water gurgling from a tastefully placed fountain, a beautiful painting, and a carefully crafted Communion table are all means of changing the stage week to week. Long before Ginghamsburg sported a megastage and the means to design sets, our weekly practice was to create a freshly designed "altar" of sorts.

Aesthetically Inviting Altars

One of my first (and favorite) altar designs included an organic version of "God's Toolbox," a long rough-hewn wooden box stocked with the tools I presumed Jesus might use to pull off some of those really tough miracles: several crusts of bread, a jar of water, some dirt in a pot, and a candle or two. In his daily walkabout journey for justice, Jesus often used the resources at hand: good old mud 'n spit, which is a simple but powerful altar display.

On another occasion our weekend message centered on our need to travel this faith journey with companions who will continually push us toward God, and we paralleled it with Dorothy's travels along the yellow brick road in *The Wizard of Oz*. Worship opened with a jazz instrumental version of "Somewhere over the Rainbow," followed by a clip from the movie and a worship leader calling us to the accountability of community. It wasn't much of a stretch, then, that for our Communion table, we secured yellow bricks assembled in a stair-step fashion with candles and Communion goblets set out on the brick "road." A pair of ruby-red slippers nearby, alongside large loaves of bread, created a storytelling display that pressed home the strength of the message, "Traveling Companions." Simply beautiful *and* simply effective.

Beautiful Stage Designs: Settings for Your Stories

A Blank Canvas

If perchance your faith community does inhabit the kind of space in which a specifically themed stage set would enhance the worship experience, I'd like to offer some of our stage designs to help get you started. It's been helpful for me as the stage designer also to be part of our worship team and hear the "heart" of each new series talked through before coming up with a design. Once we are clear on the series theme and title, our graphic designer and I partner to create the overall room ambience. It's important for the stage designs to reflect the look, feel, and colors of the series graphic.

Our best sets have always been the result of a faith-filled passion to create inspiring environments coupled with crazy ideas from just about anywhere. Let's take a tour through a few of those designs.

Modern Family

At the onset of each year, our worship team works hard to kick off January with a series that offers wide appeal to the general population. With the Christmas season behind us, we are more than ready to launch into something new, something that appeals to our sense of resolution making, fresh starts, and new beginnings. On this particular year we looked at the power and stress of relationships: how we all need help making the most of our connections with those we love. The TV series *Modern Family* was popular at the time, so we capitalized on that title and set out to design around this theme. Here's what we did stage-wise.

I decided on two key elements: large letters spelling out the title of our series, "Modern Family," in the series graphic font spread across the expanse of our stage and large empty black frames suspended above. We made patterns for our letters by printing out the title text in the same fonts as the graphic (slightly different for each word). Using an overhead projector, we projected the printout letter patterns scaled to three feet by four feet onto sheets of two-inch foam insulation available from any home improvement store. We carefully cut the letters out using our homemade version of what I lovingly refer to as our giant cheese cutter. (Search "hotwire foam cutter" online to purchase or build your own cutter.)

Several weeks ahead of time I'd put out a call to staff and servants for old frames that we could paint. We got a great response, receiving all sizes to work with. We painted all the frames and the word *modern* black but used red paint for the word *family.* Painting the sides of all the letters black really added a sharper look.

We hung the frames next, being careful to get a good left-right balance. Some frames were suspended from a PVC grid, and some were attached to the back stage wall. Whenever possible, be sure to incorporate visual depth into your design.

The letters were braced with one-inch-by-two-inch slats in back and secured to the stage floor to assure they would stay put for the duration of the series.

Right Here Right Now

Another year-opening series, titled "Right Here Right Now," was based on chapter 13 of the Gospel of Matthew, in which Jesus talks about weeds, seeds, and the "secrets" of the kingdom of God. Our worship design team wanted to make this chapter accessible and fresh to our church family. The makeover team's artist and builder, Chad Oler, came up with a way to showcase live plants. I had asked him to design window boxes and got concept drawings for much, much more. I love it when that happens!

The wall texture you see is actually window-screen mesh that can be purchased in rolls at various widths. We stapled the rolls side by side and scrunched them up a bit to catch the light and add visual texture. We then stapled these large "sheets" of screen to the back stage walls.

The window boxes are wood frames that were painted black—with galvanized steel siding cut to size by our trusty team carpenters. The windowpanes were pulled out of various barns and resale shops around our small-town communities, and we painted them in bright "seaside town" colors. We then fastened the windowpanes into various locations as seen. One of our makeover-team members is a floral designer by day and acquired more than thirty-five plants to make this design come alive! Donated vintage pots turned upside down became coasters for glass votive candles on the side walls of the worship area, where found wood-slat pieces were hung to carry out the horizontal-lined theme of the main series graphic. All together we staged a striking design to showcase a powerful series full of metaphor and visual examples—a strength for any worship environment.

The Crux

This was a Lenten message series, designed to take us deeper in faith and closer to the powerful message of the cross. We happened upon the idea of using the Latin form of the word *cross,* "crux"—the heart of the matter—thus naming this series "The Crux."

I found it interesting and visually appealing that there was a diagonal cross in the *x* of the word *crux* and began thinking about how that could play out in our stage design. I'd seen some design work done with string and a stage design done with long lines of rope. We sketched out a design, and one of our makeover servants obtained two huge spools of rope at no cost. Keep in mind that the dark background in the photos is weed cloth stapled to our back stage wall. Chemical-free weed cloth can be obtained at any home improvement store or landscape retailer and is stiff enough to work well for this application.

We started by hammering U-shaped nails onto eight two-by-four boards. For each set of stretched rope, boards were secured high and low. Each strand of rope was threaded separately and interwoven between the strands of the opposite set. The boards were painted black. Gelled lighting cans enhanced the rope angles.

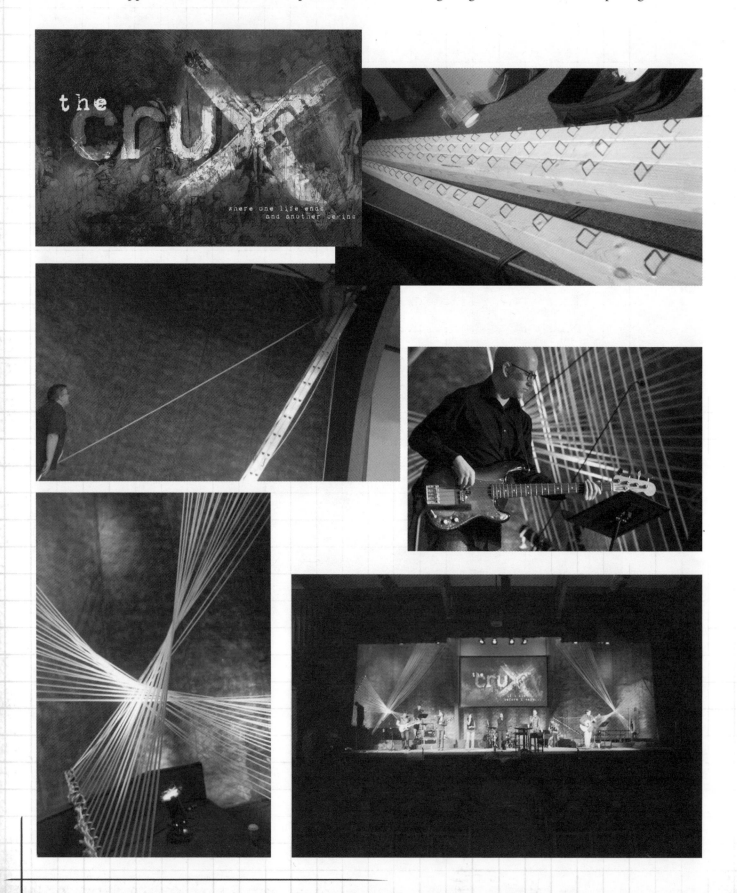

The Holy Spirit Series

For this post-Easter worship series, our team set out to design a stage to provide an engaging backdrop that reflected the look and feel of the series graphic. We were inspired by a Columbus, Ohio, Anthropologie storefront, and our key resources were clean smashed aluminum cans and paper pendant lights from IKEA. We used black-brown weed cloth as a back-wall covering, and the team hammered hundreds of cans to the wall using small nails/brads. A sleeve of one thousand can lids secured from our local Pepsi dealer rounded out the design. Finally, ketchup bottles filled with paint allowed the team to "squirt" lines of paint accents over the lids, enhancing the feeling of movement across the stage.

We lit the stage walls with our standard floor-mounted LEDs. The IKEA lights were hung from a suspended PVC grid and arranged in such a way as to mimic doves in flight across the stage. Total cost for materials and lights was $150. Special note: Our church family loved this design.

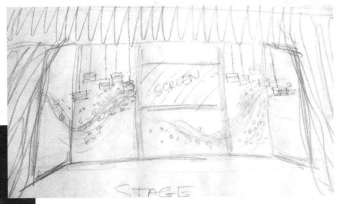

Four-Letter Words

Once the theatrical stage curtains were down (see chapter 9) and out of the way, there was good news and bad news visually. The good news was obviously a cleaner, less "boxed-in" feeling about the entire space. In addition, the beautiful wood beams that had been the underlying structural design for our worship area all along were now exposed, maximizing one of our strongest architectural features.

The bad news was that our stage had suffered a codependent relationship with those curtains. The curtains hid the side and back-of-stage space (not a pretty sight at all) and had also created a faux doorway covering at both sides of the room. We had to figure out a way to create a privacy feature for these open doorways (highly visible to the seated congregation) and an additional wall section on each side of the stage. New stage steps and a handrail for aging musicians were on the list of needs to address. As with most of our projects, we had to completely invent these solutions based on the strategic gifts among us. That is always both exhilarating and terrifying!

In the end we figured out how to build the necessary pieces simultaneously with designing a fall-series stage set. This set had a different goal in my mind, however. Rather than wanting to depict a certain series theme, I set out to maximize the brand-new expanse of the stage walls. I wanted this new set design to be a more neutral backdrop for highlighting the exciting introduction of our long-awaited no-more-stage-curtains look.

We sliced fifteen four-inch-by-eight-inch sheets of two-inch insulation foam (available at any home improvement store) into four-inch-wide lengths of eight feet (again, search "hotwire foam cutter" online for the best kind of tool). Once the foam was cut, we put down drop cloths and lined the foam lengths close to one another on the floor, where we then applied an uneven coat of paint, creating a sense of depth. This paint wasn't a solid cover but rather light and sketchy and was applied with a roller on a pole—a very important detail.

I sketched the plan for foam placement on the stage walls, and a team of three went to work measuring, pounding three-inch paneling nails halfway into the wall (roughly three per foam piece), and then pressing the foam onto the nails. Keeping a strict four inches between each length of foam was also an important detail. We did this using a four-inch piece of wood as a consistent spacer.

We filled out as much of the wall space as we could—even onto the side walls a bit—so excited to show off our expanded palette!

I finished off this stage design by purchasing a very large black shag rug for the stage floor. Rugs are typically underrated as design tools. We don't usually think of the floor as an artistic opportunity, but I urge you to rethink that notion. The floor can be every bit as important as a wall—if not more important.

In the end, it doesn't really matter whether your stage will be enjoyed by thousands or simply serve as the hub of an intimate community setting—never underestimate the power of visual display. Worshipers will focus on whatever is set before them, so use your stage to create visually

rich environments. Seize this extra opportunity to communicate the message in a different dimension. Above all, don't be afraid to try something new. Raw materials + artfully minded servants

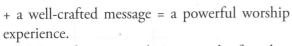

+ a well-crafted message = a powerful worship experience.

More of our stage designs can be found at www.redesigningworship.com. In addition, I often find inspiration from other church-stage designers at www.churchstagedesignideas.com.

Chapter 11

COURAGE FOR THE MISSION: WHAT IS IN YOUR HAND?

Then Moses replied, "But what if they don't believe me or pay attention to me? They might say to me, 'The LORD didn't appear to you!'" The LORD said to him, "What's that in your hand?"

—Exodus 4:1-2

Ultimately, whether you're called to design an entire worship space for thousands of seekers or simply to say a prayer for a team member, chances are there's a fear factor involved. Call it a lack of confidence or an abundance of anxiety, but whenever you and I step out to attempt great tasks, there will be a certain amount of doubt in our abilities to achieve the desired results.

Strangely—considering the large amount of redesigns I've tucked under my belt—I still experience a certain amount of fear and doubt when embarking on a makeover project. In those moments, I "feel the fear and do it anyway," certain that what God has brought me to, God will bring me through. Sounds clichéd? Hey, I can't help it; it's the truth! Take Moses, for instance.

Moses was chosen by God for one of the most monumental leadership tasks of the entire Old Testament. An Israelite by birth, Moses had been raised as an Egyptian. This gave him the perfect "crossover credentials" to succeed in delivering God's chosen people from slavery. The only trouble with Moses was inside Moses himself. He didn't realize how uniquely gifted he was, nor did he recognize the power of God being offered to him in the deal. Moses was full of excuses for why he couldn't pull off the PROMISED LAND PROPOSAL.

Excuses are nothing new. Obstacles are nothing new. All the biblical "movers and shakers" had them. Our challenge is to move over, around, or directly through them as God leads. At first, Moses saw only obstacles to the mission. When he tried to look ahead, he saw only his own low self-esteem, lack of the right social connections, and fear that the Israelites wouldn't believe that God had sent him.

I've had my own set of excuses. I've even spiritualized them at times—excuses as to why God could use others much more effectively. Here's my "short list" (I'll spare you the long one):

- I'm not particularly left-brained, and my creative right-brained tendencies can be limiting in certain structured scenarios.

- My dad was mentally ill, creating a dysfunctional and at times abusive childhood environment.

- I'm a female (and came to faith in a denomination that refused to recognize females as leadership material).

- I'm a small person (easy to be underestimated).

- I didn't pursue a traditional form of higher education.

- I'm not ordained clergy.

How's that for starters? How ironic that my path would lead me straight into a church whose empowerment theology has challenged every one of my excuses!

I love what Helen Keller had to say about excuses and challenges: "I thank God for my handicaps, for through them I have found myself, my work, my God." And God is the ultimate overcomer, who stands poised and ready with resources to help us past the obstacles. In Exodus 4:2, God asks Moses the powerful question: "What's that in your hand?" It's a personal gift–inquiry question as well as a great place to start when seeking to remodel, repurpose, and redesign spaces.

What is in *your* hand? What is it that you already have that is familiar to you? It's your tool of the trade, your long suit, and your strength. It's your best thing. You can always count on it to come through for you. What is in your hand? *Play to your strengths.* God turned Moses' familiar walking stick into a powerful snake when Moses threw it down, and when Moses picked it back up, God transformed that snake into the tool that would lead many toward their hopeful future. God asks us to throw down before him the most familiar tools from our hands and then pick them back up again with a new vision of powerful use for God's rebuilding purposes.

And on a wider scope, what has God put in your church's hand? A beautiful old sanctuary? A unique urban setting for your ministry? A parking lot large enough for a holiday festival? A donated cappuccino machine begging to supply coffee to seekers in your lobby? What is in your community's hand?

I urge you to consider the power of what is in your hand and then to trust God to maximize and empower what you find to use. In my hand is my ability to see things before they're reality, my generous and talented set of artists and builders who make up the Ginghamsburg makeover team, and the trash-to-treasure materials we drag in to work with. Most of all, as humans created in God's image, we all have in our hands the power to dream and explore, to push out beyond what we see in front of us, and to ask, "What if?"

Years ago I was rearranging the furniture in our living room—again—and feeling fairly pleased with the new "look." As I put the final pieces in place, I realized we were one side table short of a full setting—no more tables to be found. Intuitively, however, I sensed that there was a table in the room but that I just hadn't found it. Sounds crazy, I know. I gave it some time, and awhile later, after a good ideation session, it occurred to me to open the camelback trunk I'd previously lined with a fabric print. Once I opened the trunk, I pictured a piece of wood large enough to sit across the top of the open body of the chest. I walked out to our garage workshop to retrieve the right-sized piece. My husband helped paint the wood and notch out the back to accommodate the hinges and voilà. We had our missing side table, a really beautiful open-chest table that served us for many years in various locations.

What does this story have to do with anything? It validates my last favorite design mantra: **Everything you need you already have.** Deep down, because of the empowerment and resources of our Father God, I do believe that everything I need I already have. My reach, my influence, and my resources go much further as each day I wake up and thank God that everything I need has already been provided.

You, too, will encounter many moments of "lack"—that is, lack of teammates, lack of time, lack of resources, and even lack of ideas. I've been there, too. After having done everything you know how to do, you pray, and you give it a few moments. You trust God to work, and the provision will appear.

I know the difference the right setting creates for our spiritual interactions. I hear bits of feedback all the time—people thank me for the fresh designs and tell me what our teamwork means to them and their faith journey. As I bring this writing to a close, I'd like to share one note I saved. It was written after we held a special Ash Wednesday worship at our Tipp City campus. We had completely rearranged the room to provide a stage on the floor in the center of the room and seating "in the round." It was not an easy project for our media, audio, music, and design teams, but we kept in mind that "the mission of Jesus is often messy, costly, and inconvenient" (Mike Slaughter). Here is an e-mail I received subsequent to that evening's worship:

Kim,

I can't quit thinking of the service last night—so unique. I was amazed at the incredible ambience of the sanctuary. From the seating to the lighting to the music to Pastor Nick speaking from the floor [and] talking among us. If that service didn't touch hearts I am not sure what would. Nick is a gifted speaker—what a powerful message. Hearing it once was not enough.

I really don't have enough words in my vocabulary to describe how I felt as I sat in my chair trying to take it all in. In fact I am all teary-eyed just thinking about it. Thank you, thank you, design team. It was just awesome.

I love this church.

God Bless

As you embark on your own journey toward redesigning spaces in your church setting, I encourage you to be faithful and intentional and to use the gifts and skills God has put in your hand—moving forward with this promise from the book of 1 Corinthians 2:9: "God has prepared things for those who love him that no eye has seen, or ear has heard, or that haven't crossed the mind of any human being." Amen.